10 things

i wish i had known
when i started in

youth
ministry

10 things

i wish i had known when i started in

YOUTH MINISTRY

Revellyn Pletcher

ABINGDON PRESS
Nashville

ten
things
TEN
THINGS
ten
things

Ten
THINGS

ten
things

ten
things

ten
things

TEN
THINGS

ten
things

Ten
THINGS

ten
things

ten
things

ten
things

TEN
THINGS

ten
things

Ten
THINGS

ten
things

ten
things

contents

ten
things
TEN
THINGS
ten
things
TEN
THINGS
ten
things
ten
things
ten
things
TEN
THINGS
ten
things
TEN
THINGS
ten
things
ten
things
ten
things
TEN
THINGS
ten
things

Acknowledgments

Thank you to my professors: Ed Trimmer, Bill Benfield, and Kathleen Kilbourne, who got me started on this journey; to my parents: Robert Pletcher and Lynda Cook Pletcher, for their love and support; to Brandon Dirks, who helped me brainstorm the initial idea; to my church members and staff, who provided many listening ears and much encouragement; and to my friends: Ryan Thomas, Jennifer Bowden, Sarah McKinney, Doug Watts, and so many more, who believed in me and my ability to do this project. This is dedicated to all of you, and in memory of my grandmother, Mary Reuille Pletcher, who would have loved to have seen this completed. I love you all!

foreword

I started in youth ministry at the same time I started my Master's degree in Christian Education. Although I had been very active as a teen in my local youth program, I majored in biology in college and then received a master's in genetic counseling. After pursuing that career path for a year and a half, I realized God's call and became Director of Youth and Program Ministries for a United Methodist church in Elkin, North Carolina.

Two months later, I began taking classes at Pfeiffer University to get a better understanding of what a good Christian educator should do and be. I found wonderful classes and excellent theories but found that I was still missing some of the practical how-to information. A classmate and I even joked about doing our own class on all those practical things that no one ever taught in class. That joke turned into a master's project and then this book.

When I began to think about this project, I decided to get input from fellow Christian educators in western North Carolina. I took a list of potential topics to a large group of my peers and surveyed them about what their top priorities were when they started in youth ministry. I was reassured that some of the difficulties I had faced getting started were not that unusual. The initial list of fifteen topics became a top ten list, which became the subjects for my master's project and the chapters for this book.

My hope is that this how-to guide can help many starting out in youth ministry. You may know the theories about *how* to be a good Christian educator and youth pastor but, at times, still feel at a loss. Books are available on dealing with difficult people or maintaining positive discipline in the classroom, but how do you apply that to your church and its members? Here are ten possible answers. May they help you as much as they have helped me.

ten things
TEN THINGS
ten things
TEN THINGS
ten things
ten things
ten things
TEN THINGS
ten things
TEN THINGS
ten things
ten things
ten things
TEN THINGS
ten things

The past few summers, I have taken the youth on a mission experience in western North Carolina. As part of the mission week, each day starts with "Morning Watch," a solitary time with devotions prepared by the camp staff for each adult and youth camper. The Watch consists of a written devotion, Scripture readings, and prayer time, giving us the chance to start our day in God's presence and with God's Word.

As we go throughout our day on the various job sites, we keep in mind that we are there to do God's work. We start and end our work time in prayer with the person, family, or agency for whom we are working. This keeps us in touch with God's presence and reminds us of our purpose. Our goal is to meet not only physical needs, but also emotional and spiritual needs. Often, this results in our being touched by those same people.

After the workday, each night has some type of worship focus. In worship we are reminded again of the importance of God in our lives, of God's choosing us as God's children, and of the love God has for us. The week of mission is not just a time of physical work in a community, but also spiritual growth and development in the campers, both youth and adults.

It is easy in such a setting to have daily time with God. Devotional time is built into the schedule each morning. Worship time is planned each evening. But in our day-to-day life, our schedules are easily disrupted and taken over, interfering with our time with God. Early or late church meetings are scheduled, family situations arise, crises happen in the church. In my ministry, I quickly learned that it takes effort to keep that special time with God, an effort that is not only necessary, but has tremendous results.

1 how to continue your personal spiritual growth

Take Time to Care For Your Own Soul

An important aspect of the Christian educator's or youth minister's job is the nurturing of souls, helping people in the church grow and mature in their faith journeys. Unfortunately, while tending to the needs of others, we sometimes neglect our own spiritual needs. We forget that it is just as important (if not more so) to nurture our own soul as it is to nurture the souls of others. If we are not in a right relationship with God, how can we possibly serve others and model a Christian life for those who look to us for guidance? If we do not regularly find the time to be in God's loving presence, how can we possibly share that love with others? We encourage others to make regular time for God but feel hypocritical when we do not do the same. We wonder how we can possibly fit in time for God on our never-ending to-do list.

Essentials for Your Soul

⭐ Quiet time

⭐ Service to Others

⭐ Spiritual Friends and Christian Community

⭐ Time Apart

Although many Christian practices nurture the soul, here are four that will get you started. To ensure that you are growing in your walk with God, you need to make time for the practice of quiet time, acts of service, a relationship with a "soul friend" and a Christian community, and Sabbath time. All you need is the

one
ONE
one
oNe
one
one
one
ONE
one
oNe
one
one
one
ONE
one
oNe
one
one

ONE

one

oNe

one

one

one

ONE

one

oNe

one

one

one

ONE

one

oNe

one

one

one

ONE

one

oNe

one

one

one

willingness to continue to learn and grow in faith. Singly, each of the practices nurtures and develops one part of your spirituality. As with a physical meal, to have balanced spiritual nutrition, you need more than one kind of food. Together, these practices create and strengthen a close, intimate relationship with God and with your world.

In the Great Commandment, Jesus calls his followers to "love the Lord your God with all your heart, and with all your soul, and with all your strength, and with all your mind; and your neighbor as yourself" (Luke 10:27, NRSV). The two go hand in hand. By loving your neighbors, you show love to God. In loving God, you cannot help but love your neighbors. However, just as any other love relationship, you must work to strengthen it.

Quiet Time

> Very early in the morning, while it was still dark, Jesus got up, left the house and went off to a solitary place, where he prayed.
> (Mark 1:35, NIV)

Quiet time is an essential starting point for strengthening your relationship with God. It should include prayer time, Scripture reading or devotional reading, and a time of reflection. Communication is important to any relationship, especially in your relationship with God.

Prayer

Prayer is one way you can communicate with God, but it can also be a way for God to communicate with you. You will undoubtedly approach your quiet time with burdens on your heart. Of course, you will want to pray over those burdens. But do not forget to spend some time simply listening for God's voice. Meditate on your favorite Bible verse, and let God speak to you through it.

Scripture and Devotional Reading

God will also speak to you through the Scriptures and devotional books. This kind of reading will not only give you a deeper understanding of your faith, but the words will stay on your heart and give you something on which to meditate throughout the day.

Scripture is another way that God communicates with us. Too often we view prayer time as our time to unload on God, without stopping to hear what God has to say to us. Scripture helps us hear with our hearts the words of God.

To be most effective, Scripture time needs a plan. Randomly opening the Bible may bring you to some interesting passages, but it will not help you understand the context of those passages. You may choose to follow a lectionary-style plan, work your way through a book of the Bible, or find some type of devotional book that will guide you through Scriptures. This is a time for you to figure out the meaning of the passage. What is God saying to you? As you study, you will find that you will have more understanding to share with your youth as you teach.

In the back of this chapter, you will find instructions for practicing *Lectio Divina,* an ancient form of praying the Scriptures. *Lectio Divina* (divine reading) is a way to experience the Scripture or devotional passage.

Reflection

One way to spend time in reflection is by journaling. Writing down your thoughts and prayers keeps your mind focused on your time with God, instead of letting it wander onto the tasks of the day. Another way to reflect on your time is to simply contemplate the ways in which God has spoken to you and how you will intentionally apply your learnings.

Journaling about what you find in the Scripture passages not only allows you to describe what is in your heart and on your mind, but also helps you pause and reflect on the day. Writing forces you to slow down, to think about what you are reading, to concentrate and focus, and to process what you are thinking. Writing gives you something that you can come back to, to look at later on, to see how or whether your thoughts and your relationship with God have changed. Through the process of journaling, you can see God at work in your life and in your prayers.

ONE
one
oNe
one
one
one
ONE
one
oNe
one
one
one
ONE
one
oNe
one
one
one
ONE
one
oNe
one
one
one

ONE

one

oNe

one

one

one

ONE

one

oNe

one

one

one

ONE

one

oNe

one

one

one

ONE

one

oNe

one

one

one

Timing

Quiet time (morning watch, daily devotions, or bedtime prayer) is a way to refocus and center your life each day. It is also an intentional act of deepening your relationship with God. The daily discipline of quiet time does not have to be long. Even though ten minutes can seem like an insignificant amount of time to squeeze out of your schedule, it is better than no time with God. However, when you have a regular quiet time, you will find that your desire for more time with God will grow, causing your amount of time to increase as the practice is continued.

Something will always keep you busy, and the magic starting time will not occur on its own. You have to make it happen. All relationships take work, whether with friends, spouses, children, or parents. No relationship happens all on its own, including a relationship with God.

Checkpoints

❑ Take the time to center your heart and focus on God.
❑ Make your time a conversation with God.
❑ Develop a closer relationship with God.
❑ Pray.
❑ Read Scripture or devotional passages.
❑ Reflect through journaling or contemplation.

Even though you may feel that you simply do not have enough time in the day, how you spend your time each day is your choice. You choose to make that phone call, watch that TV show, or even hit the snooze alarm one more time. Your choices reveal a great deal about your priorities. Starting new habits can be difficult, but it is possible. You were not born with the habit of brushing your teeth each morning, making your bed, or cleaning out the cat's litter box; but these are all patterns you established and continue as a part of your daily routine.

Someone once said that it takes three weeks to establish a new habit. Add quiet time to your daily routine, and it will become a natural and important part of your day. People who practice the discipline of a daily devotional time describe a feeling that things do not feel right if they miss that time with God. What a wonderful problem: to miss God's presence, just as God surely misses your presence.

Jesus felt the need to spend time alone, praying and talking with God. You should as well. Conversations with God do not have to be flowery or complicated. They can be even a time of silence, listening for what God has to say. Each time Jesus was faced with a decision, he withdrew and spent time alone in prayer.

At some point each day, you should withdraw and spend time alone with God. Some people find that it helps them start their day, while others find having time at the end of the day to review the day with God is more helpful. A strong relationship is based on communication between the parties. Prayer time is communication time with God.

Service to Others

> So if I, your Lord and Teacher, have washed your feet, you also ought to wash one another's feet. For I have set you an example, that you also should do as I have done to you.
> (John 13:14–15, NRSV)

Another way to deepen your relationship with God is through service. You take your youth group on mission trips and bring them back changed in spirit, but how about your spirit? You spend so much time worrying about the details and organization of the trip that you never get around to thinking about what it is you are doing, and who you are doing it for. Your youth return changed, and you come back worn out from the experience. Service should give you a sense of purpose and a feeling of joy and contentment at the end of the day.

We have a model of servanthood in Christ, as well as his command to serve one another. Service is both a necessary part of a spiritual life and a way to grow closer to God. Jesus sent us into the world to care for one another. Service to others is a way to follow Jesus and renew our spirits. Jesus modeled for us a lifestyle of servanthood, which we, in turn, should model for those around us. You are a role model for many people, and your lifestyle is often an example for others. When you commit your life to serving others, you model for your youth what it means to be Christian. Your life can be an example for them and a way for them to identify the potential for servanthood in their own lives.

ONE
one
oNe
one
one
one
ONE
one
oNe
one
one
one
ONE
one
oNe
one
one
one
ONE
one
oNe
one
one
one
ONE
one
oNe
one
one
one

ONE

ＯＮＥ

oNe

one

one

one

ONE

ＯＮＥ

oNe

one

one

one

ONE

ＯＮＥ

oNe

one

one

one

ONE

ＯＮＥ

oNe

one

one

one

Checkpoints

❏ Serve others in response to Jesus' commandment.
❏ Model a lifestyle of servanthood for your youth.
❏ Find a sense of purpose in life through serving others.
❏ Take local and overseas mission trips.
❏ Serve others through the little things.

Get involved in service projects where you are not in charge. You need time to be in service to others, without worrying about the pastor's son falling off the roof or the amount of water being used in water fights during the car wash fundraiser. You need time to just "be" in service without feeling the sense of responsibility that usually accompanies most mission trips and service projects. Participating in (as opposed to leading) these experiences allows your soul to be touched in the same ways that you try to create for others.

Trips to other countries or other areas of this country open your eyes to new cultures and new environments as well as expand your awareness of the needs and joys of all types of people. Many times, you will return from mission projects changed, realizing that you were helped as much as those you had been helping. As almost everyone who has been involved with mission projects knows, the work you do is secondary to the relationships you build. You see God in the faces of all people, and your soul is truly refreshed.

Being in service does not always involve mission trips to foreign countries or even to places out of town. Opportunities for service in your own neighborhood do not take much time but produce amazing results. Tutoring at the local junior high or high school is a service. Organizations such as Habitat for Humanity need people not only to help with building houses, but also to raise funds for those projects. Local food pantries, soup kitchens, homeless shelters, nursing homes, and hospitals all need volunteers; and all are places where you can be in service without going far from home.

Service can even be in your own front yard. God told us to "love our neighbors as ourselves" (Luke 10:27), and you can do that in simple ways. While you may think nothing of sowing $1.97

worth of flower seeds, an elderly neighbor watching the flowers sprout, grow, and bloom may see many days brightened. Pulling the weeds out of sidewalk cracks is a service to someone who is unable to stoop to remove them. Raking leaves for a busy single mother can give her a respite and enable her to enjoy time with her children. Even though these little things may not feel like true mission or service projects, you are doing something outside of your church and outside of your job that makes a difference to someone. Anyone who has been on the receiving end of such small blessings knows how much they mean.

Spiritual Friendship and Christian Community

> The LORD God said, "It is not good for the man to be alone. I will make a helper suitable for him."
> (Genesis 2:18, NIV)

In the Creation stories of Genesis, God describes the different parts of Creation as "good." However, there is one time when things are "not good": when God realizes that the man is alone. The same is true for you in your ministry. You simply should not be alone in your spiritual life. You need other people to help nurture your soul.

Poet John Donne asserted, "No [one] is an island"; and although he did not direct his comment specifically to those who work in the church, his assertion certainly does apply. Just as you develop and encourage a community of faith for your youth groups, you need the same for yourself as well. You need other people in your Christian walk. The Lone Ranger was not truly "lone"; he had Tonto. Jesus did not do his ministry alone; he had a group of disciples around him at all times.

Spiritual friends are important and are found in many places. They may be in the church; but they may also be co-workers, neighbors, former or current classmates, or simply friends who have the ability to help you nurture your faith. Your larger Christian community is made up of spiritual friends who nurture you, guide you, and provide you with support and accountability for your spiritual journey. Spiritual friends help keep your focus on God.

ONE
one
oNe
one
one
one
ONE
one
oNe
one
one
one
ONE
one
oNe
one
one
one
ONE
one
oNe
one
one
one

ONE

one

oNe

one

one

one

ONE

one

.oNe

one

one

one

ONE

one

oNe

one

one

one

ONE

one

oNe

one

one

one

Checkpoints

❑ Look for spiritual friends in your Christian community.
❑ Surround yourself with Christian friends.
❑ Confide in your spiritual friends.
❑ Ask them to hold you accountable in your faith journey.
❑ Seek their guidance on your journey.

A spiritual friend is a confidant, a person in whom you place trust, with confidence in knowing that whatever you express will stay between the two of you. We all need at least one spiritual friend outside our church to whom we can express our frustrations and from whom we can receive objective opinions. That person eventually helps us become objective as well and encourages (even prods) us to look at a situation in a new light.

A spiritual friend may be a mentor or a guide. For those just starting in youth ministry or Christian education, a mentor may serve not only as a guide or source of advice, but as a person who can help you nurture your own spiritual development. Even long-term youth workers need someone who can do the same for them. You need a colleague outside of your own church who can be an objective listener to your frustrations and joys, and who can remind you of the true purpose of your job.

We all need someone to help us remain accountable to our walk with Christ. A mentoring spiritual friend is not afraid to tell you when you have messed up and when you are neglecting your spiritual growth. A mentor is a person who guides you by walking with you. What a true description of a spiritual friend!

Spiritual friends have a mutual friendship in which they support each other. They walk with each other and help each other by looking at life situations from different perspectives. They turn to each other for support and comfort. Spiritual friends know the inner secrets of the heart: the fears and hopes, the dreams and desires of each other. Because of that closeness, spiritual friends can have discussions that get to the heart of the issue—whether that issue is personal or spiritual. That closeness means that the spiritual friend knows what is going on in the other person's life and can honestly help him or her process and deal with problems and concerns. They help keep each other focused on their relationship with God.

Time Apart

> Remember the Sabbath day by keeping it holy. Six days you shall labor and do all your work, but the seventh day is a Sabbath to the LORD your God.
>
> (Exodus 20:8-10, NIV)

Perhaps the most difficult part of continuing your spiritual growth is taking time away to renew yourself. You may feel that you are simply too busy and cannot possibly take time away from your busy schedule for time with God. You convince yourself that the church would fall apart if you were not in your office.

We all need time apart, a Sabbath time for our souls. Our role model, Jesus, did the same thing. How many times is he described as "going away by himself" to pray and to be with God?

Take time to leave the church building behind and, if possible, even to leave your home. Home can sometimes have too many other distractions: your "to do" list, the telephone, family responsibilities. Separating yourself from these things gives you the opportunity to focus on whatever it is that you choose (a new book, other hobbies, exercise) that brings you peace and relaxation.

Checkpoints

❏ Take time away for renewal, for rest, and for refreshing your soul.
❏ Fulfill God's command to take time for Sabbath.
❏ Take some Sabbath time with your family.
❏ Take a daylong or weekend retreat.
❏ Schedule a Sabbath day as a day off.

Avoid Burnout

Just as you look to Christ for your role model, others look to you. If your own spirit is not refreshed and alive, how can you expect to refresh and enliven others' souls? You must take care of your own soul, to guard your away time, so that you can continue your spiritual growth.

17

It is very easy to work seven days a week in church work. You work on Sundays and frequently on all five weekdays, leaving only Saturday, which you quickly fill with other youth activities. Burnout does not take long, working at that pace. For your own sake, and for the sake of your family and your ministry, you must take time for yourself.

Without taking time to rest, you will not only burn out, but you will become ineffective in your job, at home, and in your personal life. Even when it feels as if you do not have the time to rest, you must. Otherwise, everything else you are doing will suffer. You need the time to renew your body, mind, and spirit. Those who look to you as a role model will appreciate that you take care of yourself. You are setting a better example by taking time away than by overworking.

Choose Your Own Sabbath

God commands us to take Sabbath time. God intended Sabbath not only as a day of worship, but also as a day of rest. For those who work in a church, worship and rest usually happen on separate days. You join in corporate worship on Sundays, but Sunday is anything but a day of rest. For those in church ministry, Sundays are the day for working long hours—morning, afternoon, and evening. Even your worship time tends to be work focused. Either you have a leadership role during the service, or you are dealing with work issues before and after worship time. Yet God instructed us to keep the Sabbath holy.

One alternative may be to have another day in the week as your Sabbath. God does not tell us that Sunday must be our Sabbath day. For those of the Jewish faith, Sabbath is sundown Friday to sundown Saturday. Likewise, you may choose another day to be your Sabbath day.

Having another day as a Sabbath day does not mean that you spend that day running errands and doing chores around the house. God intended the Sabbath to be a day of rest. One advantage of taking a Sabbath day during the week means that your children and spouse may not be at home, leaving you with a day to rest and spend on yourself. The phone may ring less often, as others do not expect you to be home. If that is not the case, turn the phone ringer off. When Saturday rolls around, you will have already had a day of rest; and you will be ready to have high-quality time with your family.

At other times, you may find that your days off are still not Sabbath time. You may find that you need a daylong or weekend retreat on your own or with fellow Christian educators or youth ministers. Time away with your peers can be refreshing and relaxing, as you share ideas and hints for spiritual growth and renewal. Regardless of where your time apart occurs, Sabbath time alone with God is important.

The Need for Spiritual Growth

The alternative to growth is stagnation. Your spiritual growth is an important but often neglected part of your life. As a Christian educator, you are called to educate those around you about the importance of attending to the spiritual life. As a youth worker, you are to minister to others but not at the expense of your spiritual needs. Remember to nurture your relationship with Christ so that you feel his love and others see him in you. Quiet time, service, spiritual friends, and time apart are ways to continue to learn and grow as you attempt to continue your spiritual growth.

Lectio Divina Explained

Reading: Slowly read the passage, repeating the parts that speak to your heart at this time.

Meditation: Lovingly repeat the text you have internalized and allow it to interact with who you are: your past, present, and future.

Prayer: Let the text become a way to offer to God your hopes and concerns and lead you into a conversation with God.

Contemplation: As you feel called to do so, rest silently in God's presence and let go of the text that brought you there.

TWO

TWO

TWO

two

two

two

TWO

TWO

TWo

two

two

two

TWO

two

TWo

two

two

two

When recruiting volunteers, timing can be everything. When I first moved to my current church position, I began looking for adult volunteers to expand the adult leadership team beyond the one couple who helped at that time. I found a woman who had a dynamic personality and an open and engaging manner with teenagers; but when I approached her a few short months after I started the job, she politely turned me down. I was disappointed but looked elsewhere and found other excellent counselors. However, I kept her in the back of my mind.

Four years later, the youth ministry had grown to the point that the junior high and senior high groups could finally be expanded into two groups; and I again needed to expand my adult leadership team. Of course, I again thought of this woman; faced the fear of being rejected; and at an open house for mutual friends, cornered her on the stairs. To my surprise and joy, this time she agreed.

What made the difference? Several things. First, she had four years to see how the youth ministry was run and to become comfortable with me and my style. I was no longer an unknown. Second, she was shortly to change jobs, from one with a lengthy commute to one that was closer to home, with fewer "take-home" responsibilities. Third, she had been moved by the recent youth-led worship service and was feeling the call to be more involved at the church.

In other words, now was the right time to invite her to join the youth ministry team. Granted, I did not know all of these factors when I asked the second time; but I certainly saw the result. For her, the timing was right the second time—to the benefit of the ministry of the team.

how to find and keep volunteers

two
TWO
TWO
TWo
two
two
two
TWO
TWO
TWo
two
two
two
TWO
TWO
TWo
two
two
two

Establish a Healthy Ministry Team

Let me guess: You truly love your job. You feel a strong sense of call to be in youth ministry. You are overwhelmed by the amount of work it takes to nurture a thriving ministry. You need help. All of you reading these words know the feeling.

Aside from the legal implications of being the only adult in a room full of teenagers, the actual ministry part of "youth ministry" will get lost quickly in the shuffle if you try to be all things to all people. A ministry team will help you become the effective youth minister you were meant to be. But a healthy ministry team does not happen by chance; it takes careful planning and recruitment as well as careful efforts by the youth ministry team leader to help the volunteers know that they (and their spiritual growth) are cared for and valued.

You cannot realistically do it alone. You cannot be in more than one place at a time. And as exciting as it is when the youth group grows, it also means that your ministry team needs to grow. Even though you would like to be able to have one-on-one time with each and every youth, the truly important thing is that each youth is in close contact with some Christian adult, that each young person feels the presence of an adult who cares about him or her.

A familiar image of a youth worker tends to be young, outgoing, athletic, and energetic; however, not all youth workers fit this description—and that is OK. A variety of different personality types exist among youth, so your youth ministry team needs adult volunteers of varying personality types. Youth will gravitate toward adults with whom they feel most comfortable, often with those who are most like them.

TWO
two
TWo
two
two
two
TWO
two
TWo
two
two
two
TWO
two
TWo
two
two
two
TWO
two
TWo
two
two
two

Essentials for a Ministry Team

⭐ High-Quality Adult Volunteers

⭐ Seeking and Finding

⭐ Training, Training, Training

⭐ Encouragement and Appreciation

High-Quality Adult Volunteers

> But the LORD said to Samuel, "Do not consider his appearance or his height, for I have rejected him. The LORD does not look at the things [people look] at. [People look] at the outward appearance, but the LORD looks at the heart."
>
> (1 Samuel 16:7, NIV)

In recruiting adult volunteers for a youth ministry team, the first step is to identify what you need and expect from the volunteers and to compose a job description. Having a thorough description of what being a volunteer in the youth ministry means will help persons understand what you are asking of them. It also means that the youth ministry leadership team will have common goals and vision because their tasks are committed to paper.

Identify the various categories of volunteers you need. For instance, you may have some great teachers who do not have the experience to cook for a large group. You may have some who are great as mentors, cooks, drivers, and administrators but not strong as teachers or small group leaders. Be clear about what you need, and fill in volunteers based on their gifts.

A job description is just as important to the volunteer as the volunteer application is to you. (See the following chapter for more discussion on this topic and information on how to write a volunteer job description.) Job descriptions are essential for volunteers. Without them, volunteers become unsure of their role in the ministry team or of your expectations. Miscommunication quickly leads to frustration on both sides. He or she may begin to feel that the commitment was more than was bargained for, and you will not be able to understand the volunteer's lack of enthusiasm. A clear description of expectations and responsibilities from the beginning can head off potential problems.

What We Do not Want to Believe About Volunteers

In an ideal world, once the job description is advertised, adults will line up to be a part of the team. Unfortunately, that is not always how it happens. However, you still need to be selective. Do not let desperation cause a choice that you, the youth, and their parents will later regret. A warm body is *not* better than nothing. Choosing inappropriate persons just because they are interested is a potential disaster. Understand that some persons want to become involved for the wrong reasons. Determine who those people are and thank them for their response to your need, but help them realize that they are not ready to be a part of the youth ministry team. By doing this, you are looking out for the best interests of the youth and the adult volunteer applicant. Parents trust you with their sons and daughters. Be honored by this trust, be in awe of the gifts placed in your hands, and be responsible in your care of the youth.

Checkpoints

❑ Be selective when choosing adult volunteers.
❑ Look for those who will help teenagers grow spiritually.
❑ Look for those who will provide a safe place for youth.
❑ Provide a job description.
❑ Have interested members fill out applications and be screened.

Volunteers as Spiritual Leaders

You want volunteers who have a sense of their own faith, who are comfortable sharing and modeling their faith, who enjoy being with teenagers, and who recognize that they have been called by God to be a part of youth ministry.

Although all Christians face times of struggle and clarification in their spiritual lives, someone with a mature faith is more likely to share his or her faith with others. Teenagers need to see someone who can model a Christian walk and is who willing to talk about how that walk affects his or her life. In the world of teens, being different is not always desirable. Seeing adults comfortable with their faith can help them to be more willing to show their own faith.

In addition to being open about their walk with God, a youth worker should genuinely enjoy teenagers. This is not always an easy task—teenagers are not always lovable people. Teens can be moody, unpredictable, critical, and awkward. Despite all of that, youth workers have to love youth.

TWO
two
TWo
two
two
two
TWO
two
TWo
two
two
two
TWO
two
TWo
two
two
two
TWO
two
TWo
two
two
two

TWO

two

TWo

two

two

two

TWO

two

TWo

two

two

two

TWO

two

TWo

two

two

two

TWO

two

TWo

two

two

two

Those who love youth love them no matter who they are and what they do. Loving youth and feeling called to be in youth ministry requires time, good listening skills, and the ability to be non-judgmental. While you cannot be in youth ministry without loving youth, you can love youth without being called to be in youth ministry.

Seeking and Finding

> "So I say to you, Ask and it will be given you; search, and you will find; knock and the door will be opened for you. For everyone who asks receives, and everyone who searches finds, and for everyone who knocks, the door will be opened."
> (Luke 11:9-10, NRSV)

In searching for adult volunteers, you will want to find someone who understands the team approach to youth ministry. Each volunteer is as important as the next, whether he or she is the newest or oldest member, he or she is leading or participating in programs, or he or she is involved in all aspects of the ministry or only one.

Invite—do not recruit—each volunteer to be a part of the youth ministry team. Although the words *team* and *recruit* go together in sports; when it comes to ministry, that changes. People like to be *invited* to things; most people do not like the idea of being *recruited* for service.

Checkpoints

- ❏ Focus on being part of the ministry team.
- ❏ Invite persons; do not recruit.
- ❏ Encourage current team members and youth to identify potential volunteers.
- ❏ Remember that student leaders can be volunteers.
- ❏ Do not overlook or overuse parents.

Who May Volunteer?

Finding great adult volunteers for the team can be a difficult task. An extremely qualified adult could be present in the front pew, and you may not even know it. Regardless of the size of the church, knowing the spiritual gifts of every member of your congregation is difficult. But other adults may know of another member's abilities.

If existing adult leaders assist in the search for new members of the ministry team, their involvement in other areas of the church (for example: members of the choir, men's groups, or women's groups) will help them find potential leaders whom you might miss.

Adult volunteers may be any age. Youth may feel a special connection with an older member of the congregation who could be a valuable asset to the ministry team but who may have been previously overlooked. Some adults may worry that they cannot relate to teenagers, or they may feel that they would not be wanted or liked by youth. However, if one of your teens asks an adult to volunteer, those fears will be put to rest. The simple fact that a youth is asking the adult assures the adult of his or her ability to connect with teenagers. Youth will think of adults whom they know and like. As mentioned before, a variety of adults are needed to match with the diverse characteristics of teenagers. If a variety of youth suggest possible adult volunteers, the range of characteristics of the adult volunteers will broaden and correspond to the youth in the group.

You probably have some youth with potential for student leadership within the group. It may be best to use college age or high school students with junior high groups and not place them in a position where they have authority over their peers. Student/adult teams may work for a youth group, with both members of the pair having a leadership role. Training and job descriptions are just as important for student leaders as they are for the adult leaders.

Having parents as leaders can be a difficult balancing act. In some cases, parents can work with youth and be welcomed by their son or daughter. Other times, having their parents involved with the group is the last thing the youth wants. Usually communication is the way to solve this problem. If one of your youth shows real concern that his or her parent has up-front leadership, consider asking that parent to volunteer in areas with minimal direct interaction with his or her son or daughter. Each family situation is different. Discuss the parent's involvement with the parent and youth, separately, to determine the true feelings of both.

Final Steps to Welcoming Volunteers
Once potential adult volunteers have been found, you should have them fill out an application and undergo screening. You may be tempted to install someone quickly in the middle of the

TWO

TWO

TWo

two

two

two

TWO

two

TWo

two

two

two

TWO

two

TWo

two

two

two

TWO

two

TWo

two

two

two

youth ministry team once he or she expresses an interest, but that response could be a mistake. Without your knowing someone and his or her background well, the members of the youth group could be put in contact with someone who may not be able to help them in their faith journey. Many churches have a risk management policy in effect that requires a background check on all volunteers in children's and youth programs. Some policies include answers to the following questions:

• Does someone need to be a church member before he or she may become involved in youth ministry?
• If so, how long should he or she be a member before applying for youth ministry?
• What references are needed to make a decision about this person?

Training, Training, Training

> For the LORD gives wisdom; from [God's] mouth come knowledge and understanding. . . . Then you will understand righteousness and justice and equity, every good path; for wisdom will come into your heart, and knowledge will be pleasant to your soul.
>
> (Proverbs 2:6, 9–10, NRSV)

Once adult volunteers for the youth ministry team have completed the process of application, screening, and acceptance, how do you nurture them as team members? In essence, this is a two part question: How will you keep them excited about being a volunteer; and how will you attend to their spiritual, emotional, and physical health?

The first thing that all volunteers—even the veterans—need is training. If all volunteers attend the same training event, they are more likely to have the same vision for the direction of the youth ministry and to understand it. Training is a good time for everyone to express expectations and specific roles and responsibilities. Both volunteers and the youth coordinator have certain assumptions about each other, and training can be an excellent time to talk about those thoughts. (Job descriptions come in handy here.) Volunteers are more likely to stay involved if they know exactly what is expected of them and if they feel capable and competent to do the job being asked of them.

Checkpoints

- ❏ Help the entire team catch the same vision.
- ❏ Determine your volunteers' areas of specialty.
- ❏ Have current adult volunteers mentor new adult volunteers.
- ❏ Provide volunteers with continued growth opportunities.
- ❏ Lead some ministry team training periodically.
- ❏ Take your team to an local, state, or national youth ministry workshop.

In addition, training events can be a time of team building within the group as old and new volunteers come together to learn and to exchange ideas. Adults who may not know one another well can meet and learn how their different personalities and leadership styles can work together for the good of the group. Veterans can mentor the new adults, sharing wisdom and understanding about the youth, the youth coordinator, and the ministry. Training can be a time for the adult volunteers to discover their spiritual gifts and areas of specialty within the ministry. The more outgoing, musical adults may be perfect for the worship team; while another adult could be your next small group leader. They will undoubtedly have gifts that they are unaware of, which could be used to benefit not only the ministry, but their own spiritual growth.

Adults need the opportunity to grow. It has been said that the alternative to growth is stagnation, which you certainly do not want in your adult volunteers. Continued workshops and training events can help the adult volunteers expand their skills and grow in their comfort level. Yearly training sessions can help the volunteers continue to grow spiritually and in their leadership skills. While a newcomer may not be comfortable leading an intense discussion on his or her faith journey, veteran adult leaders may look forward and want the chance to take on more responsibilities.

Adult volunteers need to be encouraged to grow in their own spiritual journey. Often, we focus so much on the faith development of the youth that we neglect the spiritual growth of our adult volunteers. In addition to regular prayer, personal devotions, and private Bible study, such experiences as Christian Believer, DISCIPLE Bible Study, Companions in Christ, and Sabbath retreats can nurture their spiritual growth. A spiritually healthy adult helps create a spiritually healthy youth ministry and is a powerful example for youth to follow in living their faith and continuing to grow.

TWO
TWO
TWo
two
two
two

TWO
TWO
TWo
two
two
two

TWO
TWO
TWo
two
two
two

TWO
TWO
TWo
two
two
two

TWO
TWO
TWo
two
two
two

Do some research on the best regional workshops, statewide training sessions, national retreats, and local church training events that you have the resources to attend. Your volunteers will come to understand the broader nature of youth ministry and build peer networks with other adult volunteers. They can also learn new ideas and current trends in youth ministry, facilitating the implementation of those into the local church.

Encouragement and Appreciation

> We always give thanks to God for all of you and mention you in our prayers, constantly remembering before our God and Father your work of faith and labor of love and steadfastness of hope in our Lord Jesus Christ.
>
> (1 Thessalonians 1:2-3, NRSV)

Volunteers need encouragement and appreciation. Everyone loves to be told thank you and to have his or her work acknowledged. Celebrate your volunteers. Thank them for an excellent program, for their time, for their commitment. Make certain they know that they are appreciated. Recognize and uphold the importance of their families and their personal lives. While adult volunteers may be committed to the ministry, remember their need for family time. You may be able to take a separate day off to compensate for the Saturday white-water rafting trip, but your volunteers are giving up their valuable personal time—time they may normally spend with their spouses and children. Where possible, include their spouses and children in a program or a trip. These opportunities help the youth to learn more about the adult volunteers, to feel more comfortable with them, and to build a stronger relationship with them.

Never underestimate the power of the written word. Just as the youth's accomplishments are printed in newsletters and flyers, do the same for the adults. The youth will enjoy seeing the other aspects of their adult leaders' lives, and the adults understand that their achievements and accomplishments outside the church are recognized as well. Do not forget to include another part of their personal lives—their birthdays. Include the adults' birthdays on the calendars, along with the youth's; and make sure that they are on the birthday card list.

Plan periodic appreciation dinners for the ministry team. These dinners may be a formal restaurant dinner or a youth-served meal at the church. In addition, plan some one-on-one time with each volunteer. Plan individual lunches out, or plan to brown bag it at the church. The important part is that a time is created where the your volunteers can share joys and concerns in a relatively private setting, when they know that they have your full attention. Make sure they know that you are accessible and available to help with resources, support, a listening ear—whatever is needed from you.

In addition to individual time with the volunteers, plan some type of public recognition for the adult volunteers. Thank them publicly in the church newsletter and recognize them during a Sunday morning worship service. A youth ministry team is made up of many people: Sunday school teachers, youth group leaders, supper cooks, and retreat counselors. All of them need to be recognized and thanked. Our mothers were right: Saying thank you and sending thank-you notes are important.

Checkpoints

❑ Help volunteers know that they are valued.
❑ Recognize volunteers' "other life."
❑ Recognize volunteers as individuals.
❑ Make one-on-one time for volunteers.
❑ Send written acknowledgments of your gratitude.
❑ Recognize volunteers publicly.

Sounds simple, doesn't it? Simple yet so critical. As professional youth workers, we are constantly reminded that youth ministry is relational; we need to establish and build that relationship through support, presence, and acknowledgment of important events in the youths' lives. The same holds true for your relationship with the adults. They need your support, encouragement, and appreciation just as much as your youth do.

Even though these tips do not guarantee that adults will line up at your door to be a part of the youth ministry team, these guidelines give a direction for finding adult volunteers. However, finding volunteers is only part of the process. Once volunteers are found, you must continue to nurture their physical, emotional, and spiritual well-being. Otherwise, those same volunteers will quickly become lost. Finding spiritually healthy adults is important for the youth ministry; keeping them that way is just as important.

THREE

three

THREE

three

three

three

THREE

three

THREE

three

three

three

THREE

three

THREE

three

three

three

When I was younger, my mother was a volunteer Christian educator in a church notorious for recruiting people to fill various leadership roles by saying, "We need you to do this, but it does not require you to do much." The result was that, with no clear idea of the tasks and responsibilities for the position (for example, a children's Sunday school teacher), people quickly became frustrated and did not stay long in the position. Frequent absenteeism was always a problem, often the curriculum and other resources were not fully utilized, and sometimes people were put into positions not suited for their gifts and abilities. The situation was not good for anyone—the students, the teachers, or the church.

In her professional life, Mom was writing job descriptions for volunteers in the school system, and she thought that job descriptions could help at the church as well. The education committee had the typical fears that no one would volunteer when he or she found out what was actually involved. But since she felt that the situation could not get any worse, Mom put together job descriptions for the volunteer positions.

The result was that people did volunteer. Job skills could be matched with members' gifts so that the "right" people could be recruited, and members would feel fulfilled in their roles. Volunteers also knew what was expected of them in their positions. The quality of teaching improved as curriculum was discussed in the job description and training seminars were held. Volunteers could even be involved at different levels (for example, as an associate teacher as well as a full teacher). With the teachers and associate teachers, less absenteeism occurred. The situation changed into a much better one for everyone.

how to write a volunteer job description

Clear Up Confusion About Responsibilities

> Nevertheless, in church I would rather speak
> five words with my mind, in order to instruct
> others also, than ten thousand words in a tongue.
> (1 Corinthians 14:19, NRSV)

Although Paul may have been a bit harsh toward those who were speaking in tongues, you can make the same point regarding volunteer job descriptions as well. A simply worded explanation of volunteer roles and responsibilities can go much further than a wordy and confusing document. You might as well be speaking in tongues.

Have you ever started a job and had no clue what you were getting into? You know your hire date and the job title, but you have no idea what the details of this new job are. You don't know to whom you are to report; you don't know what your supervisor's expectations are. In short, you seem to be expected just to figure it out as you go along.

Maybe you have never started a job under those circumstances, but adult volunteers for the youth ministry team begin this way on a regular basis. Too often, volunteers start their work with the ministry team with only a verbal description of what to expect. They receive minimal information and nothing in writing to help them understand what being part of a youth ministry team means. As discussed in the previous chapter, not having a clear description of expectations and responsibilities is a fast way to lose the volunteers you have worked so hard to find.

Writing a Good Job Description

A well-written job description needs five basic components: the mission statement of your youth ministry, a clear, concise job title

three
THREE
three
THREe
three
three
three
THREE
three
THREe
three
three
three
THREE
three
THREe
three
three
three

THREE
тнгєє
THRee
three
three
three
THREE
тнгєє
THRee
three
three
three
THREE
тнгєє
THRee
three
three
three
THREE
тнгєє
THRee
three
three
three

and definition, a list of expectations, clearly stated roles and responsibilities, and a basic idea of what the volunteer will get out of it. Each of these should fit with the youth ministry's mission statement, which should also plainly appear on the job description.

What are the tasks of this job? What will be the roles and responsibilities of the volunteer? How much time will it take? If the position has several responsibilities, which is to be the primary focus? How should the time be divided? What gifts or characteristics is the volunteer expected to have to fulfill that role? What are the other expectations? What can he or she expect from the church and from the youth coordinator? Who is to be his or her support or resource person? A good job description answers these questions. Be clear. Say what you mean, and mean what you say.

Essentials for a Job Description

⭐ **The Mission Statement for Youth Ministry**

⭐ **Job Title and Definition**

⭐ **Expectations**

⭐ **Roles and Responsibilities**

⭐ **Support Persons for the Volunteer**

The job title should be simple and self-explanatory. If the description is for a van driver, then that is the job title, not a "transportation engineer" or a "vehicular transporter." If you need someone to help lead weekly programs, the title is program leader. What should appear next is how this person's role fits with the mission statement of the youth ministry. If the mission or purpose statement is "to help young people grow in their spiritual journey while learning to share the good news of Christ with their friends and the community," how is the program leader expected to fulfill that statement? For example, one idea might be: "The Program Leader will lead programs that will encourage young people grow in their faith, while continuing to reach out to others." Again, a simple statement is most effective.

Next should be the general responsibilities of the volunteer and the expectations of the youth coordinator. For example, what exactly is expected of the program leader? Is she to create and lead every weekly program? Is he to work with a team of program leaders? What kind of programs is she to come up with? What should be included in the programs—music, worship, games? With whom should he work to find appropriate resources?

If a responsibility seems unclear, explain it. If the program leader is to attend monthly youth ministry team meetings, is he to report to, or to receive feedback from, the group? If you are emphasizing relational ministry, what kind of time do you expect her to put in outside of the weekly program to build those relationships? What other expectations do you have of the volunteer, not just for the specific job, but as a member of the youth ministry team?

Checkpoints

❑ Ensure that everyone is on the same page.
❑ Ensure a clear understanding of the responsibilities.
❑ Match the gifts of your volunteers to specific roles in your
    ministry.
❑ Explain the time involved.
❑ Explain the tasks involved.
❑ Explain your expectations.

What kind of gifts and characteristics are expected from the volunteer? A van driver should be a considerate driver, with an excellent driving record, but he probably would not need to be an administrator. A program leader needs to be able to relate to and shepherd youth, but her gifts would not necessarily need to include the ability to write a budget (although being a good steward of resources might be part of the job description!)

What general characteristics are expected from all volunteers within the youth ministry team? As mentioned in the previous chapter, some of these gifts can be determined during training, or through the volunteer's application. Again, if expectations are clearly spelled out in the job description, the adult who knows his or her gifts may know which area of ministry for which he or she is best suited.

THREE
three
THREE
three
three
three

THREE
three
THREE
three
three
three

THREE
three
THREE
three
three
three

THREE
three
THREE
three
three
three

THREE

THRee

THRee

three

three

three

THREE

three

THRee

three

three

three

THREE

three

THRee

three

three

three

THREE

three

THRee

three

three

three

Volunteers may have many questions, including

- To whom should the volunteer turn for support and assistance?
- What can the volunteer expect from the other adults and from the church?
- Will there be training?
- Will there be the opportunity for growth and change?
- Will there be encouragement for the volunteer to develop his or her own faith and continue on his spiritual journey?
- What resources are available for the volunteer to use?
- How does the ministry team work together?

Before problems arise, the volunteer needs to know what the steps are to deal with them and that he or she has support. Volunteer support also includes training. Again, training is crucial to help the volunteer feel equipped for his or her role in ministry.

The job description does not have to be elaborate. In fact, simple, clear statements will work better than essays describing the responsibilities, characteristics, and mutual expectations. Balance generalities and open-ended statements to cover a variety of circumstances, yet enough detail that the volunteer understands what is expected as well as what he or she can expect.

Regardless of how detailed (or how general) the statements, some kind of volunteer job description is a must. With a job description, volunteers have a sense of the mission and direction of the youth ministry. With a job description, both you and the adult volunteers have a better understanding of one another's roles, responsibilities, and expectations. With a job description, volunteers know who their support is in their ministry. You expect a job description when you are hired as the youth minister. Provide the same for the volunteers on the ministry team.

Sample General Youth Counselor Job Description

THREE
three
THRee
three
three
three
THREE
three
THRee
three
three
three
THREE
three
THRee
three
three
three
THREE
three
THRee
three
three
three

First Church
111 Main Street
Anytown, USA

Youth Counselor Job Description

First Church Youth Ministry Mission Statement
To help young people grow in their spiritual journey, while learning to share the good news of Christ with their friends and the world.

The Definition of a Youth Counselor
A youth counselor at First Church will help young people grow in their faith, while continuing to reach out to others to create a relational ministry.

General Responsibilities of the Youth Counselor
A strong youth ministry team needs committed adults who genuinely care about youth and ministry—adults who are willing to show their commitment through their time, their attention, and their own growth.

To What Are You Committing?
- Attending weekly programs consistently. (You are asked to arrive at least 15 minutes early and stay at least 15 minutes after. These extra minutes become key times for building relationships with youth.)
- Nurturing youth during the week (Follow up with them through notes, phone calls, e-mails, visits to their sports events)
- Participating in occasional weekend events, overnight retreats, ski trips, white-water rafting trips, and so on
- Assisting in planning programs and occasionally leading as needed
- Working with other youth counselors and the youth director as a team to create a healthy, relational youth ministry
- Attending a monthly youth council meeting to discuss plans for future programs and the health of the ministry
- Growing as a minister

THREE

three

THRee

three

three

three

THREE

three

THRee

three

three

three

THREE

three

THRee

three

three

three

THREE

three

THRee

three

three

three

A Few Keys to Help You Develop as a Minister

Patience: Building strong relationships with the youth takes time.

Participation: The more youth activities you experience the stronger your relationships with the youth will become.

Practice: The more you put into it, the more you will get out of it.

What Youth Need From Caring Adults

Youth ministry is not based on programs but on relationships. The most effective way to influence the youth is through significant relationships with key adults in their lives. (Do you remember an adult who had a significant impact on your life while you were a teenager?) One way to help the youth find these significant adults is to develop adult leaders who truly minister to youth, reaching them in their world, helping them learn and grow on their faith journey.

Youth Need Adults Who Will

- Love God and live for God
- Be interested in their lives
- Take the initiative to spend time with them
- Pray for them
- Be real
- Say encouraging words
- Believe in them
- Laugh
- Meet them where they are
- Remember their names and care for them
- Share God's love through personal experience
- Be consistent to the programs
- Be patient
- Enjoy life

THREE

three

THREe

three

three

three

THREE

three

THRee

three

three

three

THREE

three

THRee

hree

three

hree

HREE

hree

THRee

ree

hree

three

A Youth Counselor (or Mentor) Is:

- A friend who laughs, cries, questions, dreams, and prays with youth
- An example who teaches by demonstration not by lecturing
- Open and honest about his or her past, present, and future
- A listener—more willing to listen than to talk
- Encouraging and affirming of the best in others
- Caring—builds trust by creating a safe place to talk
- Prayerful—realizes that it is God who does the work of changing lives

What You Can Expect From the Youth Director and the Church

Youth ministry is important to the life of this church! Consequently, you can expect nurture and support from not only the church staff, but also the church members. This support is physical, emotional, and spiritual, and includes:

Accountability

A challenge to develop your ministry

Encouraging words

Leadership

Open lines of communication

Prayer

Structure

Support and direction

Training and learning opportunities

We are glad that YOU are a part of this youth ministry team!

FOUR

Four

FOUR

Four

FOUR

four

FOUR

Four

FOUR

Four

Four

four

FOUR

Four

FOUR

Four

FOUR

four

A fellow Christian educator spent a summer in college as an intern for an active youth ministry. Upon arrival, she found that several counselors were available for the summer. One, however, had a maturity level equal to the younger high school students. When he helped with the Sunday night activity, the program quickly became noisy and chaotic. However, he was good at leading the youth choir. The youth enjoyed choir, enjoyed singing, and performed well.

Obviously, this counselor's gifts were with the choir and not as much with the weekly programs. So what to do?

The easy way out would have been to ignore the situation and head back to college in the fall; but that would not have helped the intern, the youth ministry, or the other counselor. Instead, the intern decided to address the problem and find a solution. She spoke with the counselor, addressing her need for his help in keeping the youth ministry fun yet under control. They also spoke about his gifts and strengths in leading the music program. They decided to introduce music into the weekly program, allowing him to lead and giving him a cue to rein in his excitement and exhibit some self-control.

They tried this method for the last half of the summer, and it worked. The counselor was able to refocus his energies by using his musical gifts and felt affirmed because he could contribute in a positive way. The youth also benefited by the introduction of music into the whole ministry. At the same time, weekly programs went better, without as many disruptions and distractions.

I don't know whether the youth ministry continued this method after the intern left; but while she was there, the ministry flowed more smoothly. She said that she was glad she addressed the situation, rather than ignoring it, and thought that everyone benefited from the new style.

how to help volunteers find new areas of ministry

four
FOUR
four
FOUR
Four
four
four
FOUR
four
FOUR
Four
four
four
FOUR
four
FOUR
Four
four
four

Realize When Gifts Do Not Match Tasks

So you are going along in your ministry and are supported by a great team of adult volunteers, each of whom has been through application and screening. Everything should be fantastic, right? Unfortunately, that is not always the case. Even with the best process for finding just the right volunteers, you may encounter people problems.

What do you do when the ministry team is not functioning well together? What do you do if a particular volunteer seems to be in the wrong place, or if there is a conflict of personalities between members of the ministry team? You do not want to hurt anyone's feelings or make volunteers feel undervalued, but how do you help them find new areas of ministry when this one just is not working? And is there any way to head off some of these problems before they start?

Even with your best plans, the matches between volunteers and youth ministries can go astray, and you will realize that the gifts of the volunteer do not match what the ministry needs. As regrettable as this is, you can prevent it. If preventive measures are not enough, open discussions, factual communication, and even a reassessment of spiritual gifts and interests may help volunteers find an area of ministry that is suited to them.

Essentials for Helping Volunteers Find New Areas of Ministry

⭐ **Preventive Measures**

⭐ **Open Discussions**

⭐ **Confrontation With Love**

⭐ **Gifts in Other Areas**

FOUR
Four
FoUR
Four
Four
four
FOUR
Four
FoUR
Four
Four
four
FOUR
Four
FoUR
Four
Four
four
FOUR
Four
FoUR
Four
Four
four

Assessing the root of the difficulties helps not only the current volunteer, but also future ones. Identify whether or not your own behavior is causing the problem. You may need to change the way you interact with the volunteers to keep similar incidents from happening in the future.

Understanding what to do when difficulties arise is just as important. Every ministry team will occasionally run into some problems. However, when, if not before, the problem becomes damaging to the ministry, you will need to take action.

Preventive Measures

> There is a time for everything, and a season for every activity under heaven.
> (Ecclesiastes 3:1, NIV)

Setting Time Limits

Potential difficulties can sometimes be prevented. Setting up preventive measures within the volunteer job description and the volunteer process can help. Establish time-limited yet renewable job descriptions. Create a "time for everything," a beginning and an end. A well-defined job description with specific start and end dates enables both the volunteer and the youth minister to have an escape route if the situation is not working. If the present arrangement is working, the relationships are strong and healthy, and the volunteer is contributing to the growth and health of the group, the agreement can be renewed.

Having definite ending times on the job description may have the side benefit of actually increasing the number of available volunteers. Sometimes people are reluctant to volunteer because they assume that they are signing on for life. Beginning and ending dates give them a sense of participating for a season in time, with the flexibility to continue as they choose.

Checkpoints

❑ Set specific volunteer time commitments that are periodically renewable.
❑ Schedule three-month evaluations.
❑ Have new volunteers help occasionally before becoming part of the team.

Evaluate

Another preventive measure is to set a three-month evaluation meeting with each volunteer. In the business world, a review after the first three months of work is standard procedure. Adopting this procedure for the church can be just as useful. A three-month evaluation is a set-aside time for both you and the volunteer to provide support and encouragement for each other and to discuss potential improvements to the whole program. It gives the volunteer a safe place to ask for help and for you to provide the support that might turn a potentially bad situation into a successful one.

A three-month period gives the volunteer time to determine whether this particular ministry matches with his or her gifts and gives the youth minister time to determine whether the ministry team is running smoothly. Like the defined ending in a job description, a three-month review provides a way out for everyone if the situation is not working.

Allow for a Trial Period

Volunteers may find it helpful to test out the job before officially becoming part of the youth ministry team. If a volunteer helps as a chaperone for retreats or assists in the occasional program before entering into a weekly commitment, the volunteer, the youth minister, and the youth have the time to see whether the volunteer is a good match for the youth ministry program. This opportunity gives the volunteer a chance to see how the youth ministry program works, to see your style as a youth minister, and to see whether the volunteer can relate to the youth in the ministry.

You may think that someone is ideal; but when you can experience the adult as a youth volunteer, you have a better idea of whether that individual will work. Likewise, the volunteer may observe a few programs and realize that the youth ministry is not something that he or she is interested in committing to long term. Either way, an informal time together before starting a broader commitment can be good for both parties.

Open Discussions

> "Make a tree good and its fruit will be good, or make a tree bad and its fruit will be bad, for a tree is recognized by its fruit."
> (Matthew 12:33 NIV)

FOUR
Four
FoUR
four
FOUR
four

FOUR
Four
FoUR
four
FOUR
four

FOUR
Four
four
FOUR
Four
four

FOUR
Four
FoUR
Four
Four
four

FOUR

Four

FoUR

Four

Four

four

FOUR

Four

FoUR

Four

Four

four

FOUR

Four

FoUR

Four

Four

four

FOUR

Four

FoUR

Four

Four

four

Like the tree, we can make the fruit of discussions good or bad, depending on the discussion itself. An honest, open discussion includes both sides of the issue, truly knowing the other person, and providing support for each other. Even if the volunteer seems to be mismatched with the youth ministry, an open discussion is not a debate or a time for either the volunteer or the youth minister to chastise or criticize the other. Instead, it is a way to improve the situation.

Checkpoints

❏ Include both sides in the discussion.
❏ Reclarify the job description.
❏ Provide individual support.

In an open discussion, listen to how volunteers feel about their roles. Invite them to talk first. They may not be satisfied with their current positions and may be interested in adapting their involvement. The volunteer may realize that things are not going well and may have suggestions on how to modify his or her role. For example, one volunteer may want to work only with junior high youth; while another may wish to start a senior high Bible study. Apparent mismatches may stem from the frustration of feeling that the volunteers' gifts are not being used to the fullest potential.

If a volunteer is uncertain about his or her role in the youth ministry, this may be a time for explanation of job responsibilities and a review of the job description. Your frustration that the volunteer is not doing what you expect may be due to his or her not knowing what you need. Reviewing the job description can help clarify the situation and may even lead to a realization that the volunteer no longer feels called to youth ministry.

If the volunteer is feeling inadequate for the job but has good potential, ease fears by showing encouragement, support, and appreciation. If needed, provide resources or training. Together you can find ways to improve the situation for the good of everyone involved in the ministry. Acknowledge and take responsibility if you are part of the problem, and discuss ways you can work together to overcome the situation. Through both sides engaging in an open, honest dialogue with each other, you have the opportunity to determine what steps are necessary to make the youth ministry more effective.

FOUR

Four

FOUR

Four

FOUR

four

FOUR

Four

FOUR

FOUR

four

FOUR

Four

FOUR

Four

FOUR

FOUR

four

FOUR

Four

FOUR

Four

FOUR

FOUR

four

Confrontation With Love

> And let us consider how to provoke one another
> to love and good deeds, not neglecting to meet
> together, as is the habit of some, but
> encouraging one another.
>
> (Hebrews 10:24-25, NRSV)

Even with your preventive measures and your open discussions to improve the situation, you may still recognize that the volunteer in his or her current role is not effective in the youth ministry team. This discussion is different from the previous one in its tone but is still presented with love and concern for the volunteer. Good communication skills—verbal, nonverbal, and listening— are important at this time.

When you do have to confront a volunteer, find a place that is non-threatening. Your office or meeting room in the church may work, as long as the volunteer does not feel at a disadvantage. You may choose to go to a restaurant or coffee shop as a neutral site, or have the volunteer suggest a comfortable place. The volunteer's house is a third possible location. Knowing the volunteer well will help you find the best, non-threatening location for that individual.

Checkpoints

❑ Choose a non-threatening location.
❑ Keep the conversation factual, not personal.
❑ Recognize the volunteer's feelings.
❑ Inform the pastor and related committees beforehand.

Keep your conversation factual, not personal. You do not want the volunteer to feel attacked or to become defensive, although that may be inevitable. Begin the conversation by asking for the volunteer's input on how he or she thinks the youth ministry is going. Use active listening skills to hear accurately what the volunteer is saying. Many of the same conversation skills from Chapter 6: "How to Deal With Difficult People" (beginning on page 56) are applicable here. Although the volunteer may not be a difficult person, you still want to use "I" statements as opposed to "you" statements. Comments such as "I feel that the youth ministry may not be the best area for your gifts" are much easier

FOUR
Four
FoUR
Four
Four
four
FOUR
Four
FoUR
Four
Four
four
FOUR
Four
FoUR
Four
Four
four
FOUR
Four
FoUR
Four
Four
four

to hear than "You are not doing a very good job in the youth ministry." Use specific examples when you talk about the problems. But be sure not to turn the examples into a laundry list of complaints or trivial incidents.

No matter how delicately you approach the conversation, you can expect the volunteer to be surprised, hurt, or defensive. Keep other people's views and opinions out of the discussion. Listen to and validate his or her reactions and emotions. Listening helps the volunteer feel heard and gives him or her the opportunity to correct you if you misinterpret voiced feelings. If the volunteer is upset, allow adequate time to express these emotions. At some point, you can help the volunteer find a more suitable area for his or her gifts and talents.

As a precaution, discuss the matter with the pastor and possibly the staff-parish or related committee before speaking with the volunteer. The pastor or committee may have tips for dealing with the situation and can help determine the right course of action to take. If others know ahead of time, they will not be caught unaware if an upset volunteer comes to them. The committee or pastor will have had input into the situation and may be better able to support the decision for the volunteer to find a new area of ministry.

Gifts in Other Areas

> Now there are varieties of gifts, but the same Spirit; and there are varieties of services, but the same Lord; and there are varieties of activities, but it is the same God who activates all of them in everyone.
>
> (1 Corinthians 12:4-6, NRSV)

Helping volunteers discover their unique spiritual gifts will help them make a transition into a new area of ministry in the church. A spiritual gifts inventory for church members enables everyone to discover strengths and abilities, potentially finding new areas of ministry in which to serve. A volunteer may be pleasantly surprised to learn of gifts and strengths. Each spiritual gift is a blessing, and everyone has his or her unique set of spiritual gifts. No one person has all the gifts. Therefore, each person is needed; and each person has a place. You must all work together.

Checkpoints

❑ Provide periodic spiritual gifts inventories.
❑ Involve every church member in some form of ministry.
❑ Help the volunteer find a new ministry area better suited to his or her spiritual gifts.

Once the volunteer has determined his or her spiritual gifts and interests, it may be easy to discover which ministry area best suits those gifts. Using spiritual gifts in conjunction with likes, interests, areas of excellence, and passions can help a volunteer to find a niche. When looking for a good match for a volunteer and an area of ministry, look at all these aspects. A volunteer may be passionate about fighting illiteracy but may not have the ability to teach. Likewise, a volunteer may be very good at teaching teenagers at the local high school but have no interest in doing so at the church. To truly find a good match between volunteer and a ministry area, all of these factors must be considered.

Many churches have some way of involving each church member in some form of volunteer lay ministry. The use of spiritual gifts inventories and commitment sheets listing many possible areas of service can help the volunteer find a better match for himself or herself. If each church member understands that service and volunteer time is a ministry, he or she will have a greater perspective of what it means to be part of the church.

Helping the volunteer find a new ministry area is not simply a matter of shuffling him or her from position to position, without ever addressing any possible underlying problems. You do not want to alienate this person. After all, he or she is a beloved child of God. But neither do you want to continue to enable inappropriate or unproductive behavior. If you have had an open, honest discussion, where you have lovingly confronted the problems, and if you have assisted the volunteer in determining his spiritual gifts and best ministry areas, then you can help the volunteer find the best place for him or her to have an active, vital role in the church.

Everyone needs to be involved in some area of ministry. However, not every area of ministry is suited to every person. It is your job to help volunteers find the best area, even if it means leaving youth ministry behind. Just remember to do so in a loving way, remembering that "all the members of the body, though many, are one body" (1 Corinthians 12:12, NRSV).

FOUR
Four
FOUR
four
FOUR
Four
FOUR
four
FOUR
Four
FOUR
four
FOUR
Four
FOUR
four

FIVE
FIVE
FIVE
Five
FIVE
five
FIVE
FIVE
FIVE
Five
FIVE
five
FIVE
FIVE
FIVE
Five
FIVE
five

One winter, I looked ahead to the next year and realized that, with the large group of soon-to-be seventh graders, space was going to be a problem. Having two groups—one junior high and one senior high—is generally a good idea because of the different levels of emotional maturity. So it was a good time to implement this new practice.

In the spring, I brought to the attention of the student leadership team the large incoming seventh grade class, and they quickly voiced the same space concern I had. Since they were aware of the problem, it was a perfect opportunity to present a possible solution (splitting into two groups), involve the youth in the change process, and give them ownership of the change.

The senior high youth were in favor of the change, but the soon-to-be eighth-graders (who had been with the senior highs for a year) were not happy about being separated from their older buddies. I did not ignore their concerns but talked with them and their parents about the proposed idea. I was still not sure that those youth were entirely in favor of the proposed change; but the parents were persuaded, providing critical support. During the summer, I sent a letter to the parents and the youth, letting them know about the plan in the works. At meetings, I gave them the opportunity to raise questions and concerns.

Once the youth ministry was back in full gear in the fall, the new schedule was included with every piece of publicity that was sent home. Joint activities were regularly planned to develop fellowship among the entire group; and at student leadership meetings, we discussed how the new method of youth ministry was going. The change was not easy, and there were bumps in the road every so often; but overall, the new plan went well. The youth felt as if they were a large part of the process, making the change easier to adjust to.

how to work with people resistant to change

Implement Change Successfully

It has happened to everyone. You think you have the perfect, innovative idea that will dramatically change and improve the way you do your youth ministry. Then suddenly someone throws a bucket of cold water all over you and your idea. "But, we have never done it that way before." "It won't work." "We've already tried that." Before you throw your Youth Minister of the Year award out the window, stop and take a deep breath. Why is this person not as excited about your idea as you are?

Essential Steps for Implementing Change

⭐ Realization That a Change Is Needed

⭐ Knowledge of What Kind of Change Is Occurring

⭐ Determination of the Direct Effects of the Change

⭐ Encouragement of Others' Participation

⭐ Adaptation of the Change as Needed

⭐ Assessment of the Change

Most people simply do not like change or may not understand why a change is needed. Change upsets their routines and their created order. When things in their lives are changed, stress usually results because of the new, the unknown, the unexpected. Humans are called "creatures of habit" for a reason. Generally speaking, we like knowing what is supposed to happen day to day. Sure, we like some variety in our lives; but drastic change—

five
FIVE
FIVE
FIVe
Five
FIVE
five
FIVE
FIVE
FIVe
Five
FIVE
five
FIVE
FIVE
FIVe
Five
FIVE

FIVE

FIVe

FIVe

Fiue

FIVE

five

FIVE

FIVe

FIVe

Fiue

FIVE

five

FIVE

FIVe

FIVe

Fiue

FIVE

five

FIVE

FIVe

FIVe

Fiue

FIVE

five

that is a different story! Why do we need change? Aren't things still working without having to upset the *status quo*? Why do we need to change the way we do things?

So, how do you help people deal with the unknown—to understand, accept, and be a part of a vision for change— especially when change becomes a necessary part of the ministry?

To have a better chance at successfully implementing change, work through a process: realization, knowledge, direct effects, participation, adaptation, and assessment.

Realization That a Change Is Needed

> And the one who was seated on the throne said, "See, I am making all things new."
>
> (Revelation 21:5, NRSV)

At some time or other, everything changes. The first stage in the process of implementing change is *realization*. Often, a new and revolutionary vision may catch people off guard because they are not aware a change is needed. As far as they are concerned, everything is going well, so the *status quo* certainly does not need to be altered. They may not understand what the new vision is or the direction that the vision is going.

Checkpoints

❑ Define the needed change.
❑ List why the change is necessary.

When you introduce change, explain the rationale behind the need for the change—why it needs to happen. Do this as factually as possible. This stage is not the time for an emotional plea or for "If you don't do this, then ..." statements. This stage is the time to be non-threatening and non-emotional, to make the statements, to clarify the vision, to explain why change is necessary, and to point out what problem, need, or issue the change will address.

Knowledge of What Kind of Change Is Occurring

> Think over what I say, for the Lord will give
> you understanding in all things.
> (2 Timothy 2:7 NRSV)

Once people have begun to understand that the proposed change is important, the *knowledge* stage can begin. Again, the vision or plan should be explained in non-threatening, non-emotional language. Although more details will be explained at later stages, for now at least, the basics should be communicated. If the group has gone past the realization stage to the *knowledge* level, they will want to have a broader understanding of what the change is and the plan or vision for implementing the change. Take this time to discuss with them what together you hope will happen.

Checkpoints

❑ Explain the change.
❑ Let others know the overall vision.

At this stage, you can introduce some of the details and supporting information, although you will want to be careful not to overwhelm your team. Too much information at the beginning of the process may simply be a case of "too much, too soon." However, you will need to provide enough data so that it does not appear that key details are being hidden. Hit the highlights of what can be expected in implementing the change and vision. At these initial stages, a broader vision and picture of what is to come is better than getting into minutiae that may end up changing as the plan proceeds. Providing an excess of details at the beginning allows too many opportunities for the plan to get bogged down in discussing all of the small details. Realize that this information will need to be discussed several times, in several different formats (verbal, written, presentation) to be most effective.

FIVE
FIVe
FIVe
FIVE
FIVE
FIVE
FIVe
FIVE
FIVe
FIVE
FIVE
FIVE
FIVE
FIVe
FIVE
FIVe
FIVE
FIVE
FIVE

FIVE
F\Ve
Five
FIVE
five
FIVE
F\Ve
Five
FIVE
five
FIVE
F\Ve
Five
FIVE
five
FIVE
F\Ve
Five
FIVE
five

Determination of the Direct Effects of the Change

> I will give you a new heart and put a new spirit in you; I will remove from you your heart of stone and give you a heart of flesh.
>
> (Ezekiel 36:26, NIV)

When the people begin to react to the proposal, the *direct effects* stage has been reached. People want to know how this change is going to directly affect them on a personal level. Resistance may begin to surface. In this phase, you might start to hear, "But we've never done it that way before." People start wondering where they fit in this new idea.

You will also find that a lot of history resurfaces during this stage. Maybe an earlier youth minister proposed a new idea and did not follow through, or the idea failed. Regardless of how tempting it may be to ignore the former youth minister's difficulties or to attribute the failure to bad timing, this is still not the time for arguing. This stage is the time to listen to these concerns with active and reflective listening, to restate the information and vision, to address the concerns and to answer questions.

Checkpoints

❑ Be prepared to answer questions such as, How will this affect me?
❑ Explain how the change will affect the church.

Next, the affected area begins to expand. In addition to wondering how the change will be personal, some will question how current (or even future) programs will be affected or which volunteers or staff members will be involved. Others will want to know the involved cost and whether the funds to pay for it are available. Be prepared to answer these questions factually. Think through every possible question (even the ones surely no one would really ask) and have the answers ready. Think of a typical business manager. What are his or her usual concerns? Money, time, personnel? Be ready to respond to these concerns.

As the issues and concerns are being addressed, this is often the place where proposed changes stop. Even after a wonderful proposal with the carefully planned and organized facts and answers, the response may be an attitude of "Who cares; let it be; it has always been this way; we can wait until we really have to do this." Although you may have a great idea for building and expanding the shrinking youth group, the people hearing your presentation may not think that a change is necessary until no youth are left at all. As frustrating as it is to encounter those attitudes, your job at this stage is again to listen actively and reflectively, listen to expressed feelings, and determine the results of implementing (or not) either the initial proposal or the opposition's options.

However, if the people see the vision and get behind the change, begin gathering input on the details, continue to answer questions, and ascertain the desired end results.

Encouragement of Others' Participation

> We know that all things work together for good for those who love God, who are called according to his purpose.
>
> (Romans 8:28, NRSV)

Even though these many steps may seem like a waste of time, they are necessary before entering the *participation* stage. Otherwise, the group will repeatedly backtrack through the above steps but without the organization that could have been possible. The initial groundwork and homework are crucial. The desired change will be clear to everyone and take less time in the long run if you do the necessary preparation.

Checkpoints

❏ Be clear about how others can help.
❏ Have a plan for working together.

When participation is reached, everyone is behind the idea and ready to try it by working together. The together part is important. Everyone has been a part of the process so far and needs to continue to be a part of the process. By working together, everyone takes ownership of the vision and makes it a collaborative idea, not just yours.

FIVE

FIVe

F\Ve

Fiue

FIVE

five

FIVE

FIVe

F\Ve

Fiue

FIVE

five

FIVE

FIVe

F\Ve

Fiue

FIVE

five

FIVE

FIVe

F\Ve

Fiue

FIVE

five

As the vision becomes clearer and begins to be enacted, others will want to help. They may even want to introduce still more people to the project. As the vision becomes a reality, you must be willing to let go of your ownership of the idea and allow others to help. Your job at this point is make the idea successful by offering training, training materials, other informational resources, and support.

Adaptation of the Change as Needed

> The Spirit of the LORD will come upon you in power, and you will prophesy with them; and you will be changed into a different person.
>
> (1 Samuel 10:6, NIV)

After the proposal has been implemented, and the people participating in it have tried, tested, and used the idea for a while, they will begin to come up with different and sometimes better ways to do things. They will make it their own. This *adaptation* stage can be difficult for the originator of the vision, who has to be able to let go of his or her original innovation and recognize the validity of others' new ideas. As part of the *participation* stage, everyone claimed ownership of the vision. With shared ownership comes the shared right to make changes, whether or not these changes were a part of the original vision.

Checkpoints

❑ Rejoice when your team makes the original idea better.
❑ Keep the adapted change part of the overall vision.

Occasionally, the original proposal may appear to take a new and different direction. It is not always easy to tell what is simply different from the original plan and what may actually be a misdirection of the first vision. Just because the current direction is not what was in mind at the beginning does not mean that the new direction is wrong. However, if the idea or proposal has shifted away from the original mission statement or vision, the group may need to bring everyone back to the primary plan and vision. Often the group can determine better than one person whether the adapted change is still in line with the initial vision.

Assessment of the Change

> Every good and perfect gift is from above, coming
> down from the Father of the heavenly lights, who
> does not change like shifting shadows.
>
> (James 1:17, NIV)

The final step in the change process is *assessment*. However, even though this appears to be the final step in this particular cycle, the entire change process is truly a series of cycles, with assessment leading to a new round of realization, knowledge, and so forth. With assessment, you should hear from all the parties involved (those who are involved in the change and those who are making the change) and pull everyone together to discuss what is working, what is not working, and what needs to be adapted.

Checkpoints

❑ Ask yourself: Is our change effective?
❑ What is the next cycle of change?

This stage is a good time for focus groups, surveys, and interviews to find out whether the current form of the idea is still in agreement with the vision and intention of the proposal. If adaptations are needed, make them. However, changing the original vision restarts the change cycle. After assessment, the process starts all over again as new ideas, proposals, and changes occur. The process never ends.

What to Be Aware of

Sometimes people get stuck at different levels, whether it is at realization, knowledge, or direct effects; and it can be difficult to get them unstuck. However, the relationships among the people involved—those helping with the change, those affected by the change, and you—affect how well the change works. If a relationship of trust, credibility, a good rapport, and good communication exist among the parties, the process will work much better than if the initiator is new, not viewed as credible, or typically ineffective at communication. Have you heard the advice not to make any major changes until you have been in a

FIVE
FIVE
FIVE
Five
FIVE
five
FIVE
FIVE
FIVE
Five
FIVE
five
FIVE
FIVE
FIVE
Five
FIVE
five
FIVE
FIVE
FIVE
Five
FIVE
five

FIVE

FIVE

FIVe

Fiue

FIVE

five

FIVE

FIVE

FIVe

Fiue

FIVE

five

FIVE

FIVE

FIVe

Fiue

FIVE

five

FIVE

FIVE

FIVe

Fiue

FIVE

five

position for at least a year? This is a good example of the reason. You need a year to establish a relationship base and to do your homework so that the proposed change really does meet needs.

One variable that cannot be accounted for when planning a vision is everyday human foibles. Some people will not want you to succeed, will want to play political games, or will want to know whose "side" you are on and who your allies are. Based on these alliances, they may or may not want to help.

You may even experience professional jealousy among other staff members. They may feel that the new idea is receiving all of the attention, leaving them out of the limelight. Maybe they are watching you succeed with an idea that they were not able to get approved. So what do you do about these problems?

Unfortunately, these complications are hard to anticipate and even harder to resolve. The main thing is to be aware of and sensitive to the potential land mines of feelings and emotions and to work through them in a way that treads on the fewest toes.

One more thing to be aware of is that these same steps and dangers can apply to you when a pastor, education chair, or the deacons involves you in his or her vision for change. Think about these questions: How did you react when someone came to you with a new way of doing something? Have you been stuck at a step? Have you reacted with professional jealousy? How did the initiator of that change involve you in his or her process? How did you react to the idea of change?

Change is never as easy as you would like it to be. Regardless of how well you plan and organize, you will have some bumps in the journey that cause you to rethink and reevaluate your vision and ideas. Do not become discouraged. Even if the idea does not work at the moment you think it should, it may not be a dead issue. The timing simply may not be right. Yes, there will always be people who are not particularly crazy about you or your ideas. However, by helping people realize the changes needed, presenting the information in as factual a manner as possible, answering the management types of questions, and addressing the outcomes, you can get to the point of participation and implementation. Be prepared to repeatedly rethink, reevaluate, and reassess the vision.

Change may not be easy, but it is possible. Remember that, in nature, all things grow and change or else they die. Change is neither good nor bad; change is essential to life.

FIVE
FIVE
FIVe
Five
FIVE
five

FIVE
FIVE
FIVe
Five
FIVE
five

FIVE
FIVE
FIVe
Five
FIVE
five

FIVE
FIVE
FIVe
Five
FIVE
five

SIX

SIX

SIX

six

six

six

SIX

six

SIX

six

six

six

SIX

six

SIX

six

six

six

I will admit that I can be stubborn. (My grandmother and I called it "determined.") When confronted with a difficult person, my gut reaction is sometimes to dig in my heels and push back. Not confronting the person makes me feel as though I am swallowing my pride or giving in. I also admit that I have a dramatic personality, which can grate on some people. So I have found it necessary to tone down. It is a compromise, not a cave-in. Just as I might find someone else difficult, I am sure that others may feel the same way about me.

In one church where I worked, such a conflict arose. A coworker and I had very different personalities, which led to difficult interactions and, at times, even hostility between us. That situation could not continue as it was, so I changed my personality with that person. The conflict did ease eventually. However, it took a great deal of time, some mutual recognition of our differences, and even some intervention from a third party.

I toned down my personality and expected similar compromises from the other person. When those did not happen initially, I was faced with two choices: to continue to wait for changes that might or might not happen or to leave the difficult situation and the church. I chose to stay, to hope for change, and to pray for some type of resolution to the conflict. (I did not pray that the other person would change.)

The heavens did not open up, and angels did not come down and make a dramatic peace between us. But, over the course of two years, I learned how to gain perspective on the situation, how to let go of my irritation, and how to deal with the conflict. Are we best friends? No. Will we ever be? Probably not. Can we be civil to each other and work together in such a way that we respect one another's gifts and abilities? After some time and mutual understanding of our respective personalities, yes we can.

how to deal with difficult people

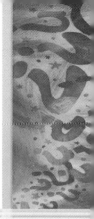

six
SIX
six
SIX
six
six
SIX
six
SIX
six
six
SIX
six
six
SIX
six
SIX
six
six

Change the Outcome of Interactions

Everyone has encountered a difficult person; and often, the human reaction is simply to limit interaction with him or her. But what do you do when the difficult person is someone you have to encounter on a regular basis? What do you do when it is the staff-parish relations chair, the Board of Deacons chair, or the pastor? These are not persons from whom you can distance yourself; but if they drive you crazy, or even worse, make you seriously reconsider your call to ministry, you have to find strategies to keep your interactions with them civil.

Essentials for Dealing With Difficult People

★ Evaluation and Appraisal of the Difficult Behavior

★ Understanding That the Other Person Will not Change

★ Separation From the Behavior

★ Development and Implementation of a Coping Strategy

★ Evaluation and Modification of the Coping Strategy

Changing the outcome of your interactions with a difficult person takes several steps. First, look at the behavior to determine seriousness of the situation. Next, realize that you cannot change the other person's behavior. You can change only your own. Separate yourself from the situation, gaining distance and perspective. Finally, review and change the strategy as needed for the next interaction.

SIX
six
S\X
six
six
six
SIX
six
S\X
six
six
six
SIX
six
S\X
six
six
six
SIX
six
S\X
six
six
six
SIX
six
S\X

So-called "difficult people" can exist in many areas of your life. In some circumstances, you can simply avoid dealing with those people. However, in your church, difficult persons are not always avoidable. You need a method of working with them in ministry, whether they are colleagues, committee chairs, or church members. Although a person or the behavior may not change, the outcomes of your interactions with him or her can be different.

Evaluation and Appraisal of the Difficult Behavior

> A soft answer turns away wrath, but a harsh word stirs up anger.
> (Proverbs 15:1, NRSV)

Interacting with people on a regular basis can be difficult for everyone. We have all had those days where the simplest thing can push our buttons and drive us crazy. We know that we have quirks and foibles that can irritate others as well. But what changes the behavior from a personality trait or eccentricity into a truly challenging situation? The situation boils down to a few basic questions: Is this person truly difficult? Who is the problem: you or the other person? Is the problem serious enough to make it worth changing your behavior or trying to change the other person's behavior?

Checkpoints

❑ Articulate your definition of a "difficult person."
❑ Determine the problem.
❑ Assess the severity of the problem.

A "difficult person" has been defined by Donald Weiss (in *How to Deal With Difficult People*, AMACOM, 1987) as someone "whose behavior regularly interferes with your ability to get along with him or her and/or get your work done effectively." The key word here is *regularly*.

Someone who is tough to get along with occasionally is not truly a "difficult person" but is someone who may simply be having a bad day (even if it happens often). Think of the legal phrase "presumed innocent until proven guilty." Has the difficult person reacted differently in a previous, similar situation? Are you overreacting to the situation? Is there a recognizable cause for the other person's behavior? Can the situation be diffused easily with simple, open communication between the people involved? If the answer to all of these questions is no, you may indeed be dealing with a difficult person.

In addition to determining whether the person is difficult, you need to assess the degree of the situation. What exactly is the problem, and how serious is it? Is it a clash in personalities or something more? Do some circumstances seem to make the situation worse or better? Even though seemingly small things can add up, creating larger problems, you may need to assess the situation realistically and determine how big (or small) the problem is. Only you can determine whether the issue is actually a problem. Everyone has different levels of tolerance. What one person cannot stand, another finds laughable. While you may think that a church member's attitude is positive, another finds his or her demeanor overly exuberant and grating. Part of evaluating the interactions with other people is determining not only what is the difficult interaction, but also determining the intensity of the problem and what your next step should be.

Understanding That the Other Person Will not Change

> Do not be quickly provoked in your spirit, for
> anger resides in the lap of fools.
> (Ecclesiastes 7:9, NIV)

Once you have confirmed that the other person really is difficult, what do you do? The next step is to stop wishing that the difficult person were different. Doing so is easier said than done. Obviously, this person does not think the way you do; or there would not be a problem in the first place. But does the fact that difficult people think differently always mean that they have to change their way of thinking? People think and react differently to the same situation, so try not to assume that someone will respond in a way that always makes sense to you. First and foremost, recognize that the other person is reacting in a way that makes sense to him or her. Everyone has past experiences and current life situations that influence his or her behavior—just like you do. Simply acknowledging some of those factors may help. The situation will not go away, but acknowledging can ease some of the frustrations.

SIX
six
S\X
six
six
six
SIX
six
S\X
six
six
six
SIX
six
S\X
six
six
six
SIX
six
S\X
six
six
six

Checkpoints

❑ Recognize differences in thinking and reacting.
❑ Realize that people do not change just because you want them to.
❑ Understand that you can change only yourself.

You may be tempted to assume that the other person should be the one to change. The reality is that the other person is probably as set in his or her ways as you are. The odds of others changing because you think that they should are pretty slim. Do not waste your energy wishing for that nonexistent change to happen— energy that could be better spent elsewhere. If the difficult people in your life always do things a certain way, do not expect that this time will be different. Just think—he or she is probably hoping that *you* will change.

You cannot change the other person; you can change only yourself. As you recognize the behavior and your reactions to it, you realize that you have to change your reactions. You cannot change the other person.

For instance, you know an eccentric, golden-hearted church member (let's call him Howard). Howard performs a lot of good volunteer work at the church. He behaves in ways that drive an entire staff crazy. He opens the church office windows when he is volunteering (even when the air conditioner is on) and rearranges the library furniture. Talking to Howard does not cause a change in his behavior. So the staff has two options: continue being irritated by him, or reconcile themselves to the fact that the windows are going to be open and the furniture rearranged and appreciate the many hours of volunteer time this man unselfishly gives to the church. Letting go of the irritation helps lower the staff's collective blood pressure and stress level. If, however, the person's behavior is affecting other members' health and safety, the situation must be dealt with, if not by the pastor, then by the appropriate committee.

Separation From the Behavior

> Everyone should be quick to listen, slow to speak and slow to become angry.
>
> (James 1:19, NIV)

Once you realize that you cannot change others, you need to separate yourself from the behavior. The behavior triggers reactions in you, which cause further actions in the other person, which cause more reactions in you, which creates a vicious cycle. Your task is to break the cycle by stepping back and gaining some perspective on both the behavior and your reactions. Through understanding the cycle of behavior, and even the origin of the behavior, you can develop an effective coping strategy for dealing with the difficult person. Eventually (believe it or not), you can gain a detached view of the person, even in the midst of an awkward situation. *Detached* does not mean that you have no feelings. In fact, it actually helps if you can see things from the other person's perspective—an empathetic reaction.

Checkpoints

❑ Understand the behavior/reaction cycle.
❑ Gain perspective on the behavior and the reaction.
❑ Let go of the irritation.

Do not perceive the behavior as being aimed at you personally. Often, many other people find the difficult person to be challenging. Most likely, he or she behaves the same way toward many people. Seeing these actions as less personal, and more of a personality trait, helps break the reaction-action cycle, and puts you into a more effective coping strategy.

Development and Implementation of a Coping Strategy

> But the wisdom from above is first pure, then peaceable, gentle, willing to yield, full of mercy and good fruits, without a trace of partiality or hypocrisy.
>
> (James 3:17, NRSV)

You have assessed the situation, determined that the person is truly a difficult person, but also recognized the limited likelihood of changing anyone other than yourself. You have broken through the cycle that seems to be caused by the other's behavior, have begun to understand the roots of the behavior, and have started taking words and actions less personally. Now, you finally are ready to develop a coping strategy.

SIX
six
S\X
six
six
six
SIX
six
S\X
six
six
six
SIX
six
S\X
six
six
six
SIX
six
S\X
six
six
six

SIX
six
SIX
six
six
six
SIX
six
SIX
six
six
six
SIX
six
SIX
six
six
six
SIX
six
SIX
six
six
six

Prayer is the first step in any coping strategy for dealing with a difficult person. However, you are not praying for the other person to change; you are praying for the situation to be resolved effectively. If you have involved other people, such as a pastor or committee chair, ask them to pray for the situation too.

Whether you would consider the difficult persons in your life neighbors or enemies, you can be sure that Jesus calls you to love them and pray for them. Prayer has to be the main focus before, throughout, and after the conflict resolution. By praying continually throughout the process, you submit your own wishes and frustrations to God and "make room" for God to work it out. When you offer the struggle to God, you can have confidence in your handling of the situation because you have handed over the reigns to God.

Pray for the right words to say. Pray for the right attitude. Pray for peace. Pray for understanding and wisdom. Pray for patience. Pray that the outcome would be pleasing to God. Pray for all of the individuals involved, that you may all discover a new way to experience the love of God as you resolve this conflict. The necessity of prayer in difficult situations cannot be underestimated.

Checkpoints

❑ Pray for the other person and for your encounters with him or her.
❑ Change your actions to improve the outcome of the interaction.
❑ Be non-confrontational.

Since you know that you cannot change the other person, you are going to have to change how you interact with him or her. If you can learn how to deal with the difficult person in a way that brings about the most positive responses from that person, your overall encounter with that person will improve. What can you do to make this an agreeable interaction? What positive interactions with this difficult person do others have that you can emulate? Your goal is to improve your interactions with the person so that the result is one you can deal with, without feeling tense or stressed.

Think through possible scenarios in which you encounter that person. Some of these may even be weekly occurrences (such as a staff meeting), so the format of the discussion may be very familiar. Consider ways to change the discussion by finding ways to make it more positive.

In addition to preparing mentally for the next encounter with this person, consider when and where to implement the new coping strategy. Try to find a time when the other person is not under unusual stress, as well as a time when your level of energy and emotional equilibrium are sufficient for trying these new tactics. Find the best time for both of you to ensure maximum success.

The place is also critical. Ambushing someone in front of a crowd will put him or her on the defensive, setting up your new plan for failure. On the other hand, the other person's behavior may be better in the presence of others than in a private, one-on-one situation. Give some thought to which scenario—private or public—will optimize your chances of a positive encounter.

Preparation and research can improve the outcome of your next meeting. Once you have figured out how, when, and where to make the encounters more agreeable, go for it. Implement your strategy.

Evaluation and Modification of the Coping Strategy

> Let your eyes look directly forward, and your gaze be straight before you. Keep straight the path of your feet, and all your ways will be sure.
>
> (Proverbs 4:25-26, NRSV)

After you have implemented your coping strategy and the ensuing encounter has taken place, evaluate and modify the strategy as needed. Any time a process is started or something new is implemented, you must review and adapt the plan, making appropriate changes. For a coping strategy to work, be prepared to employ plenty of energy, effort, and prayer.

After trying the coping strategy with the difficult person, look at the result. Did the strategy work? Did the problem get better; or was the encounter, at least, more effective or positive? If so, congratulations!

SIX
six
SIX
six
six
six

SIX
six
SIX
six
six
six

SIX
six
SIX
six
six
six

SIX
six
SIX
six
six
six

SIX

SIX

SIX

six

six

six

SIX

SIX

SIX

six

six

six

SIX

SIX

SIX

six

six

six

SIX

SIX

SIX

six

six

six

If it seemed unsuccessful, realize that your attempt to ease the situation simply may not work, or worse, could even aggravate things due to no fault of your own. Does this mean that you should not try to improve things? No, but it may mean that you need to change the strategy.

What did not work: the time, the place, the approach? Talk (discreetly, of course) to other persons who know the person. How do they have positive interactions with this individual? What suggestions do they have? Then, try again, and again, and maybe even again.

Eventually, a time may come for you to abandon your efforts for the time being or, perhaps, even permanently. As part of deciding to change and modify your strategy, you may determine that you need to get away from the person. In some cases, such as in a larger church, you may be able to limit your interactions with the difficult person. However, in a smaller church, or when the difficult person is the pastor, a colleague, or the chair of the staff-parish committee, you obviously cannot avoid him or her forever.

Checkpoints

❑ Decide whether the strategy worked.
❑ Determine how you could modify the strategy.
❑ Discern when to say, "Enough."

Unfortunately, if the coping strategy is not working after repeated tries, you may need to involve the pastor or the staff-parish chair for assistance and support. If the problem person is the pastor or the staff-parish chair, the situation is a bit stickier than it can be with church members. If the situation seems beyond repair, you may need to consider seeking a job in another church.

Your decision is a tough one. You may genuinely like your job, the other people you work with, the town, and many other aspects of your situation but feel that you need a job where you are at peace. On the other hand, you may decide that your current job is worth whatever the difficult person is capable of dishing out. You will have to determine whether you are running away from a problem that will only go with you or you are leaving to find a better situation. Regardless, you can learn something from the experience for future reference. Ultimately, only you can make that decision.

You can work through difficult situations, but realize that not everyone will love you or the quality of your work. As much as you do not like it when someone is upset with you, your mental view of that person is what matters. For your own well-being, you must decide when you are able to cope with a difficult person and when he or she is too much for you. Deciding that the person is too much to cope with does not mean that the person has "won" and you have "lost." If you diligently try the process of coping and finally gain a sense of peace about the situation, you are a winner.

SIX
SIX
SIX
SIX
SIX
six
SIX
SIX
SIX
SIX
SIX
six
SIX
SIX
SIX
SIX
SIX
six
SIX
SIX
SIX
SIX
SIX
six

SEVEN

seven

SeVen

seven

seven

seven

SEVEN

seven

SeVen

seven

seven

seven

SEVEN

seven

SeVen

seven

seven

seven

Prescription painkillers are being abused more and more often. A few years ago, just weeks before MTV and some of the major networks did special reports on Oxycontin®, our town learned exactly what this drug was and how it can be misused.

Several local teenagers were arrested for stealing, selling, and using the drug, shocking our small community. Two of them were church members, one a former member of the youth ministry. Although I was greatly saddened by the events, I realized that this was an issue that had to be addressed within the youth ministry. After spending time at the courthouse at the trials of these young adults, I knew that we needed to look not only at the drug, but also at medical and legal aspects.

I invited to the group a local doctor and lawyer, both church members known by the youth. I had a tape of the MTV special ready to play as well. But before the night of the program, much publicity already had been done. The monthly newsletter I sent to the youth was posted on the bulletin board outside my office, letting others in the church know what was planned. The weekly church newsletter also carried the information with two weeks' notice. Just to be on the safe side, I also sent a letter to all of the youth ministry parents, detailing the program for the night; and I discussed the plan with the pastor.

The program went well, imparting the medical and legal information as well as providing time for discussion about the video's content. Afterward, the presenters evaluated the program; and I answered any questions the youth had in ensuing weeks.

Talking to teens about drugs can be touchy. Some parents think that their son or daughter is not ready to hear the information. Others worry about the possible content of the discussion. With advance notice, parents can decide what they are ready and willing for their teen to hear.

how to handle controversial topics

Discuss Touchy Subjects in a Godly Manner

You feel that the time is right to introduce a topic in youth group that may raise a few eyebrows in the congregation. Maybe it is the issue of abortion, homosexuality, premarital sex, or drug use. Wherever an issue has more than one viewpoint, you will have debate and discussion. These subjects create strong emotions, so how do you present these to your youth group without the weekly meeting turning from a discussion to an argument? Just as important, how do you introduce controversial issues into your youth program without parents or even non-parental congregants deciding that you have overstepped your bounds?

Essentials for Handling Controversial Topics

⭐ **Consideration of the Youth in the Group**

⭐ **Comfort With the Topic**

⭐ **Distribution of Information to the Youth, Parents, and Church**

⭐ **Presentation of All the Information**

⭐ **Follow-up Time With the Youth After the Discussion**

Many schools include a section in their teacher training on "Controversial Issues in the Classroom." Learning from those guidelines and using simple common sense can head off many potential hazards before they take shape. As with any program you put together for your youth group, do some preliminary work; be comfortable with the topic; publicize the upcoming program; keep particular considerations in mind during the

seven
SEVEN
seven
SeVeN
SEVEN
SEVEN
seven
SEVEN
seven
SeVeN
SEVEN
SEVEN
seven
SEVEN
seven
SeVeN
SEVEN
SEVEN
seven

SEVEN
seven
SeVeN
SEVEN
SEVEN
seven
SEVEN
seven
SeVeN
SEVEN
SEVEN
seven
SEVEN
seven
SeVeN
SEVEN
SEVEN
seven
SEVEN
seven
SeVeN
SEVEN
SEVEN
seven

program; present both sides of the debate; and, of course, follow up through discussion with the youth and feedback.

Consideration of the Youth in the Group

> Each of you should look not only to your own interests, but also to the interests of others. Your attitude should be the same as that of Christ Jesus.
>
> (Philippians 2:4-5, NIV)

Before the topic is scheduled for a program, think about the youth in your ministry. The seven-year age spread is vast when it is the possible difference between a sixth grader and a senior in high school. Their maturity levels are very different; even the difference in maturity level between youth of the same grade can be immense. In addition, youth have particular home and personal situations that may affect their reactions to the topic.

Checkpoints

❑ Consider age and maturity levels.
❑ Consider personal and home situations.
❑ Consider knowledge levels.

If you keep junior high and senior high together for program time, consider separating them when you discuss difficult topics. Even if both groups are capable of discussing the same topic, they will be at very different emotional and maturity levels and will quickly get frustrated with each other's reactions to the topic.

Consider the personal and home lives of the group members. Would some youth be affected personally by this topic? While you may choose not to cancel the program, certainly keep in mind that if one of your youth has a best friend with an eating disorder, this topic could be tough for him or her. Likewise, a discussion on homosexuality may be touchy for a teenager who is struggling with feelings of being gay or lesbian or has friends or family who are. Youth may have parents whose views are very strong, and a debate bringing up oppositional viewpoints may make the youth feel awkward. Be available after the program for personal one-on-one time with youth if it is needed.

Be familiar with what most of the youth already know about the topic. Is this a topic that has been discussed in depth at school? If so, the discussion should focus more on the Christian response to the issue at hand and less on basic factual information.

Think carefully about the topic being introduced. Are the genuinely interested in this subject, or is it something that only you think they are interested in? The group will miss out on needed opportunities to grow spiritually if you limit them to the topics they want. However, you do need to strike a balance between the expressed wants and the unexpressed spiritual needs, especially when introducing a topic that is potentially controversial.

Comfort With the Topic

> Have nothing to do with stupid and senseless controversies; you know that they breed quarrels. And the Lord's servant must not be quarrelsome but kindly to everyone.
> (2 Timothy 2:23-24, NRSV)

Once a topic is chosen, you need to be familiar with what is being introduced. Whether it is homosexuality, euthanasia, or premarital sex, know the facts as well as the opinions behind the issue. Thoroughly knowing the subject matter will help your comfort level, which will help the group. The youth will know if you are uncertain about the topic, which will immediately increase their unease. Know the facts and statistics to back up each side. (Having them in writing is perfectly acceptable.) To make a well thought-out decision about a difficult issue, you must know the facts and figures behind your beliefs.

Checkpoints

❏ Know both sides of the topic.
❏ Solidify your own views.
❏ Anticipate potential questions.

You need to know your own beliefs about the topic to be discussed. While your own viewpoint may or may not come into the discussion, you still must know your stance. Guard against

SEVEN
seven
Seven
seven
seven
seven
SEVEN
seven
Seven
seven
seven
seven
SEVEN
seven
Seven
seven
seven
seven
SEVEN
seven
Seven
seven
seven
seven

SEVEN

seven

SeVeN

seven

seven

seven

SEVEN

seven

SeVeN

seven

seven

seven

SEVEN

seven

SeVeN

seven

seven

seven

SEVEN

seven

SeVeN

seven

seven

seven

allowing your opinions to become the focus in a discussion with the youth. If you are struggling with the issue, say, "I'm still working on what I think." Youth need to know that you, too, may have a hard time coming to a decision about controversial issues. Being comfortable with your own views on the issue will help your comfort level with the subject matter. For example, depending on the group, a discussion about sex may elicit plenty of giggles. If you blush while talking about the subject, you will not help matters.

What questions are the youth likely to have? Think through possible scenarios. Anticipate how you will deal with difficult questions. Be prepared to hear just about anything from youth. Whether for shock value or out of a genuine curiosity, youth ask a wide range of questions. A little forethought and preparation can save you from being caught off-guard.

Distribution of Information to the Youth, Parents, and the Church

> O give thanks to the LORD, call on his name, make known his deeds among the peoples. Sing to him, sing praises to him; tell of all his wonderful works.
>
> (Psalm 105:1-2, NRSV)

Once a topic has been selected, and you are prepared and comfortable with it, what is next? Publicity. Publicity serves several purposes: It gives the youth, their parents, the congregation, and the pastor a chance to prepare themselves for the topic and to voice comments and concerns. In most situations, publicity can help everyone be aware of what is coming, and less surprised when it actually happens.

Some youth leaders do not advertise their programs ahead of time, feeling that the youth should be present no matter the topic. This is one time when you cannot do that. Youth need to know that a controversial subject is coming up. Knowing ahead of time helps them feel that you are preparing them for a topic; and if they are uncomfortable with the subject matter, foreknowledge gives them the option of choosing not be present. Even the youth who will choose to attend may want to prepare themselves mentally and emotionally for the particular issue.

Be sure that the parents know what is to come. Send a letter to parents that states the issue and gives a brief overview of how you will approach the issue. Ask parents to pray for their teen and for you as you study the topic. Give parents some questions they can use to discuss the issue at home.

Asking the youth to tell their parents will not work. And you should not assume that the parents will read the flyer sent to the youth announcing the subject matter. That brightly colored flyer designed for refrigerator use for the entire family may well end up under the teenager's bed or lost in a pile of homework. Start the advertising with the youth and their parents weeks before the program occurs. This gives parents and youth time to come to you and express concerns and questions. Their worries may cause you to rethink your presentation of the material, or you may be able to alleviate their concerns and ease their fears.

Checkpoints

❏ Inform the youth of the topic.
❏ Inform the parents in a separate letter.
❏ Inform the church and the pastor.

Be sure that the publicity is visible in the church, on bulletin boards, in the newsletter, and on posters. You may feel that your programs are the business of no one, except the youth and their parents; but if you give open and obvious notice of what is going on, it does not appear that you are trying to hide what you are doing. In addition, do not forget to tell the pastor about the upcoming topic. If your pastor is typically unaware of the weekly youth programs, this is a time to make an exception. When the pastor knows what is being done, he or she can be an ally in case of later trouble. Plus, pastoral backing will give a little extra validity when explaining why you felt that this issue was relevant to the lives of the youth.

SEVEN
seven
SeVeN
seven
seven
seven
SEVEN
seven
SeVeN
seven
seven
seven
SEVEN
seven
SeVeN
seven
seven
seven
SEVEN
seven
SeVeN
seven
seven
seven

SEVEN
seven
SeVeN
seven
seven
seven
SEVEN
seven
SeVeN
seven
seven
seven
SEVEN
seven
SeVeN
seven
seven
seven
SEVEN
seven
SeVeN
seven
seven
seven

Presentation of All the Information

> But the aim of such instruction is love that comes from a pure heart, a good conscience, and sincere faith.
>
> (1 Timothy 1:5, NRSV)

When the time comes for the actual discussion, use the following approach. If you present your opinion, emphasize to the group that your view is not the only way. Youth need to discern a situation and set their own beliefs. Your job is to enable them to make their decisions, based on facts and on Christian principles.

Checkpoints

❏ Present all sides.
❏ Present various Christian viewpoints.
❏ Empower the youth to form their own opinion.

Present all sides of an issue, including the various Christian views, with the pros and cons of each. Youth need all of the information so that they can come to the best decision about the topic. Even if you do not agree with a particular view, present all of the information as objectively as possible. Teenagers may need some guidance in making wise decisions, but they also need to be trusted to make those decisions.

Present the many Christian viewpoints so that the youth can reconcile their beliefs about the issue with their beliefs about their faith. Because of differing interpretations, the Bible is sometimes used to support opposing views; so examine with the youth the biblical passages and their contexts. (You may want to have a concordance, commentary, and curriculum on hand.) Help the youth understand the opinions, while explaining that even Christians have varying viewpoints. This does not mean that the people on the other side of the issue are not truly Christian, but that people struggle to reconcile their views on the issue with their beliefs.

Youth are able to form their own opinions about the topic. This is the tough part. The Bible may speak to a certain viewpoint, your denomination may state another, you may believe a third viewpoint, and society may claim yet another way of looking at the

situation. All of these can be valid. While you may be tempted to state that there is only one way of looking at a topic, the reality is that teenagers receive many messages. Help the youth to be able to make a thoughtful decision on their own, with full knowledge of the arguments. If they believe a certain way only because someone tells them to, that belief will fall apart at the first testing. However, if they have reached an opinion based on understanding all of the implications of their beliefs, they are much more likely to hold to it, even under debate.

Follow-up Time With Youth After the Discussion

> Get rid of all bitterness, rage and anger,
> brawling and slander, along with every form of
> malice. Be kind and compassionate to one another,
> forgiving each other, just as in Christ God
> forgave you.
>
> (Ephesians 4:31-32, NIV)

All things have an end; but even after the program is over, your work is not. Follow-up with the youth is a must to ensure that they leave feeling good about one another after what may have been a lively debate. In addition, youth who are personally affected by the topic may need some one-on-one time to sort through feelings. Be sure that the pastor knows of situations that arose in the meeting, and be prepared for feedback from parents. Just as controversial topics are difficult to deal with during the discussion, they can remain difficult long after the program is over.

Checkpoints

❑ Remember to depart in love.
❑ Be available for the youth.
❑ Expect parental feedback.
❑ Report to the pastor.

At the end of the program, remember to end in Christian love and understanding. Controversial topics would not be controversial if they were not touchy enough to cause emotions and tempers to run high. Help the youth remember that Jesus taught us to love our neighbors and to forgive one another, just as we have been forgiven. They should not judge one another for

SEVEN
seven
SeVeN
seven
seven
seven
SEVEN
seven
SeVeN
seven
seven
seven
SEVEN
seven
SeVeN
seven
seven
seven
SEVEN
seven
SeVeN
seven
seven
seven

SEVEN

seven

SeVeN

seven

seven

seven

SEVEN

seven

SeVeN

seven

seven

seven

SEVEN

seven

SeVeN

seven

seven

seven

SEVEN

seven

SeVeN

seven

seven

seven

what they have said during the discussion, but love one another, and if necessary, agree to disagree.

Be available after the meeting to help youth work through their feelings or to answer any additional questions that they did not want to ask in front of the group. Their needs may even extend well after the program is over. Particular youth may need time to process the information they have received and will need to discuss the issue further at a later date. Others may have immediate reactions that need addressing by an adult. For that reason, having several adults on hand during the discussion is a definite plus. These adults should be the usual volunteer counselors—people the youth know and are comfortable with. Be especially aware of youth whose family or personal issues may influence their reactions. Let them know that you are available for them as well.

Expect reactions from parents. Despite the extensive advance publicity, someone may feel that he or she was not completely informed of the topic or may have a problem with the content of the discussion. Remain calm when listening to parents' worries and fears, and do your best to work through their concerns with them. Other parents may be excited and pleased with how things went, especially if a Christian understanding was put on difficult subject matter that they may not have been able to do at home.

Let the pastor know what happened during the discussion either immediately after the session or first thing the next day. If a youth was particularly disturbed by the conversations, the pastor may want to follow up with him or her in addition to your spending additional time with the youth. Further, if the pastor has been informed about what occurred at the meeting, he or she can better deal with any parent who might come to him or her with concerns. The pastor would have some knowledge of what went on and will already have heard your perceptions of the discussion. The pastor will appreciate being kept informed in case of potential problems.

Dealing with controversial issues is never easy. Not only is it difficult for the leader, trying to present information in as fair a manner as possible, it also can be difficult for youth to understand what is being presented and come to a decision concerning their beliefs. However, given ample warning, parents and youth can be ready for youth to learn about tough topics. Both you and their families need preparation time, in order for the discussion to be truly effective. With your preparation before, understanding during, and follow-up after the program, the discussion should be one from which the youth can learn and benefit.

SEVEN

seven

SeVeN

SEVEN

SEVEN

seven

SEVEN

seven

SeVeN

SEVEN

SEVEN

seven

SEVEN

seven

SeVeN

SEVEN

SEVEN

seven

SEVEN

seven

SeVeN

SEVEN

SEVEN

seven

EIGHT

eight

eIGHT

eight

eight

eight

EIGHT

eight

eIGHT

eight

eight

eight

EIGHT

eight

eIGHT

eight

eight

eight

A few years ago, while on a mission trip, a fellow youth leader told me she needed to learn from me. "I want to learn how to discipline with a smile, like you do!"

I had to stop and think about what she had said, and I realized that I do tend to discipline "with a smile" in my church's youth ministry. The group knows me well; so when I make silly and outrageous threats (while laughing) they know that: a) I love them; but b) they do need to calm down, stop talking, or stop whatever it is that they are doing.

I use a lot of humor and exaggeration when I deal with discipline issues. When youth on a retreat were sitting on a brick wall with a drop-off behind them, I asked them to get down "so you won't fall off, break your heads, die; and then I have to call your parents to let them know." We all knew that I was overstating what could happen to them, but it also told the youth what I wanted and why I wanted it.

I do not talk down to the youth; and from the beginning of the year or the beginning of any trip or event, expectations are clearly spelled out for what behaviors are acceptable and are not acceptable. Consequences are also explained at the same time. That way, everyone has the same information from the get-go. I try to remember, when all else fails, that I am in charge.

how to discipline in a christian manner

Keep the Love of Christ While Keeping Control

We have all had it happen—the night when everyone just seems a little too boisterous in the youth meeting. Maybe it was the double chocolate cake and caffeine-filled soda served with supper that night, or maybe everyone is just excited about your program on "The Christian Parallels to Marching Bands." Regardless, the group feels out of control. One boy is busy wrestling with another in one corner, while two others are describing every detail of Friday night's football game. A group of girls is dissecting one girl's Saturday night date and laughing at the wrestlers in the opposite corner. The visitors are sitting quietly in chairs by the door, looking as though they are ready to make a run for the parking lot. Although you are tempted to make a run for it along with the visitors, you know that is not an option. But how in the world do you regain and keep control of the group?

Essentials for Disciplining in a Christian Manner

⭐ Balance of Affirmations and Boundaries

⭐ Evaluation of Behavior to Determine Whether It Is a Problem

⭐ Formation of a Youth Group Covenant

⭐ Publication and Calm Implementation of Consequences

⭐ Parental Involvement

On the other hand, we have all had the nights where everything is going pretty well; but one youth just refuses to go along with the show. While independence and non-conformity is good at some times, it can be very disruptive at other times. How do you

eight
EIGHT
eight
eIGHT
eight
eight
eight
EIGHT
eight
eIGHT
eight
eight
eight
EIGHT
eight
eIGHT
eight
eight

eight

EIGHT

eight

eIGHT

eight

eisht

eight

EIGHT

eight

eIGHT

eight

eisht

eight

EIGHT

eight

eIGHT

eight

eisht

determine whether the behavior truly is disruptive, deal with it, and still claim to be a place for Christian love and understanding? Does "turn the other cheek" apply, or can you find a compromise between inaction and asking people to leave?

Disciplining in a Christian manner is not always easy. It involves a balance of affirmations and boundaries; it evaluates behavior; it involves the group in setting and implementing a *behavior covenant*; it explains and enforces consequences for unacceptable behavior; and it involves the parents. Most important, when you are dealing with discipline issues, you must act in a loving manner.

Jesus was lovingly confrontational. Although we have no doubt that he loved others, he had definite ideas about how we should live. He summed up the Ten Commandments when he said that we should love God with all our heart, mind, soul, and strength; and our neighbors as ourselves. If we truly did love our neighbor as ourselves, wouldn't our world be a different place? Although your youth group may not be quite to that level of concern for others, it is still a place for thinking about others during your interactions. When some level of concern for others is not happening in your group, then some type of correction may be needed.

Balance of Affirmations and Boundaries

> Love is patient, love is kind. It does not envy, it does not boast, it is not proud. It is not rude, it is not self-seeking, it is not easily angered, it keeps no record of wrongs. Love does not delight in evil but rejoices with the truth. It always protects, always trusts, always hopes, always perseveres.
>
> (1 Corinthians 13:4-7, NIV)

Disciplining in a Christ-like manner is a combination of affirmation and boundaries, both of which are absolutely necessary. Even more important, a balance of boundaries is crucial—not too lenient and not too strict. The first step in Christian discipline is to be positive. Set positive expectations, strongly believe in youth empowerment, and use affirmations as much as possible as youth grow and mature.

Checkpoints

❏ Set positive expectations.
❏ Empower the youth.
❏ Affirm the gifts and growth of the youth.

People, especially teenagers, live up or down to others' expectations. When you expect the worst from them, the worst is often what you will get. Instead, if you believe in them and believe that they are capable of great things, they frequently rise to the occasion. Many times, you may see great potential in one of your youth. However, that young person may be the one who interrupts the leader or always has some smart-alecky comment to make. When you place this youth in a position of responsibility—the leader of a game, activity, or program—you may recognize leadership skills that you had not seen before. If you dismiss the youth as being only a disruption, you would miss out on his or her capabilities. If, instead, you recognize potential, put it to use, and have high expectations, youth can live up, not down, to your expectations.

Having positive expectations of youth often means empowering youth as well. For example, in western North Carolina at Carolina Cross Connection, a week-long mission program, the training emphasizes to the youth that they should not just help people, but empower them as well. In the adult training, an additional form of empowerment is emphasized: empowering the youth in the work groups by encouraging the youth to try new things (even power tools), encouraging them to stretch their comfort zones, and affirming the steps they take as they grow.

The adults at Carolina Cross Connection often find that it truly becomes a balancing act, trying to keep others on the work team from getting hurt, while at the same time encouraging the youth to do what is necessary to get the job done and to try new things. Always, affirmations and appreciation were offered for whatever was being done, especially for the less than fun-filled jobs. One of the leaders realized that she had been effective when, at the end of the week, one girl declared, "Thank you so much for acting as the group's mother and as part of the gang this week. Sometimes it's nice to be independent, but other times it's nice to be looked after and know that you're loved." That is empowerment—not only to allow youth to stretch and grow in an environment where they are supported, but to encourage them to do so; not to do it for them, but to give them the abilities to do the task themselves.

EIGHT
eight
eIGHT
eight
eight
eight
EIGHT
eight
eIGHT
eight
eight
eight
EIGHT
eight
eIGHT
eight
eight
eight
EIGHT
eight
eIGHT
eight
eight
eight

EIGHT

eight

e\GHT

eight

eight

eight

EIGHT

eight

e\GHT

eight

eight

eight

EIGHT

eight

e\GHT

eight

eight

eight

EIGHT

eight

e\GHT

eight

eight

eight

Evaluation of the Behavior to Determine Whether It Is a Problem

> The LORD is slow to anger, and abounding in steadfast love, forgiving iniquity and transgression, but by no means clearing the guilty.
>
> (Numbers 14:18, NRSV)

Be sure to determine when the behavior is merely annoying, and when it is inappropriate. Although it may be tempting to view every interruption as a disruption, the boys who are wrestling and girls who are giggling before the program really are not behaving inappropriately. They are being teenagers. Likewise, some talking and whispering during the program is more annoying than disruptive. How many adults get bored during committee meetings and find other things to do while there? Is that behavior inappropriate? Perhaps, but it mostly just annoys the speaker as long as it does not distract the attention of fellow committee members. Inappropriate behavior occurs when the youth begin to be disruptive or disrespectful. That is when the disruption needs to be stopped.

A good lesson for all times, but one that especially applies here, is to avoid stereotyping youth. We have all looked at the way some youth dress and made assumptions about their behavior, either that they are a troublemakers and disruptive or that they are well-behaved and attentive. Avoid defining certain youth as problems. If you keep positive and high expectations about behavior, you will often be pleasantly surprised as the youth meet and exceed those expectations. Those so-called "problem youth" may not be a problem at all when interacting with peers at the church. If you stereotype them, you may miss out on someone who has much to contribute. Remember that people live up or down to the expectations set for them.

Checkpoints

❑ Determine whether the behavior is simply annoying or truly disruptive.

❑ Ask yourself whether you are stereotyping the youth and his or her behavior.

❑ Allow the youth to change and grow.

EIGHT
eight
eIGHT
eight
eight
eight
EIGHT
eight
eIGHT
eight
eight
eight
EIGHT
eight
eIGHT
eight
eight
eight
EIGHT
eight
eIGHT
eight
eight
eight

We can be thankful that youth do grow and mature. The boisterous junior high youth will eventually settle down and be able to focus on a task for more than five minutes. You, the adult leader, must recognize their growth and affirm their development. Positive reinforcement will go farther than continual chiding. Be sure to change your impression of and interactions with the youth as they change their behaviors. Just because a youth was quiet as a seventh grader does not mean that she will not become more outgoing as she gets older. Similarly, a youth who is overly energetic in sixth grade confirmation classes may settle down as he matures. Our perceptions of them must adapt as they change.

Formation of a Youth Group Covenant

> How very good and pleasant it is when kindred
> live together in unity!
> (Psalm 133:1, NRSV)

Unfortunately, by the time the situations described at the beginning of this chapter have started, it may be too late to start implementing new rules. To be able to truly discipline in a positive manner, certain things need to happen before the chaos starts. Another technique the staff at Carolina Cross Connection use to encourage positive discipline is to have the entire camp help set the rules for the week. They form a covenant on the first day of camp. All campers (youth and adults) then promise to abide by the covenant for the good of the community. The covenant is stated simply in short phrases and words to express what the group wants their newly formed community to be. These statements are written in positive words. In the development of the behavior covenant, the youth explain why each of the guidelines is important. The covenant spells out clearly what the consequences will be when the guidelines are not met.

Covenants should be explained from the beginning. Although you may think that a rule is understood, it very well may not be by a particular youth group member. You cannot curtail what you think is misbehavior if the youth in question does not know that it is misbehavior. When planning the next youth lock-in, have the youth discuss and develop the covenant for that particular event

EIGHT

eight

eIGHT

eight

eight

eight

EIGHT

eight

eIGHT

eight

eight

eight

EIGHT

eight

eIGHT

eight

eight

eight

EIGHT

eight

eIGHT

eight

eight

eight

several weeks in advance. Send the covenant home before the event for both the youth and the parent to sign. If the youth know from the beginning that smoking or being alone in a room with a member of the opposite sex will result in their being sent home, they are far less likely to break those rules. Let's face it, being a teenager means pushing the limits. However, they still need to know from the beginning what the limits are and what happens when those limits are pushed too far.

Checkpoints

❏ State expectations from the beginning.
❏ Use simple language.
❏ Identify the rationale behind the results.

Covenants should be stated simply. A few simple rules that are easy to remember go much farther than an endless array of "Thou shalt nots." The simpler and clearer, the better. Jesus understood that concept. While the Old Testament Book of Leviticus outlines many laws for all kinds of circumstances, and even the Ten Commandments are specific rules, Jesus summarized them in two simple statements: to love God with your heart, mind, soul, and strength, and to love your neighbor as yourself. Jesus understood that the more rules there were to remember, the harder it is to keep them all. He also knew that positive phrasing is more palatable than a list of "don'ts." Truly, short, sweet, and to the point is effective.

We do not follow rules we do not understand. (Why were we not allowed to chew gum in junior high, anyway?) When we know the rationale behind the rules, they become easier to follow. When we were children, the worst reason our parents could give for a rule was "Because I said so." It holds true for teenagers and adults as well. If part of the covenant states that you will treat one another with respect, it is because a church should not be a place for belittling or harassment, but a place of love. When you tell youth on the mission trip not to get into paint fights, they are less likely to do so if they understand that the homeowner bought the paint with money saved over several months.

Publication and Calm Implementation of the Consequences

> Instead, as he who called you is holy, be holy
> yourselves in all your conduct; for it is
> written, "You shall be holy, for I am holy."
> (1 Peter 1:15-16, NRSV)

Once you have established a covenant (that is, agreed on the rules) within your group, establish logical consequences that are known from the beginning. Again, having the youth help set these consequences is extremely important. Consequences that are established by the youth are effective. While you may be tempted to think that they will be too lenient on one another, the opposite tends to be true. They are tough on themselves. In addition, if they know that they and their peers have set the outcomes, it is easier for them to abide by the decisions. They know that you are not being unreasonable or unfair if they helped set the consequences for their own actions.

Checkpoints

❑ Get input from the youth on what the consequences should be.
❑ Be sure that the consequences are logical and worded well.
❑ Implement consequences calmly.
❑ Enforce the consequences without anger.

Your consequences should be published, just as your covenant was published, and for the same reasons. If the consequences of actions are known ahead of time, they are less likely to actually be needed.

The consequences should be logical. Consequences that are too extreme simply are not effective. If the consequences are too light, behavior can spiral out of control; while consequences that are too harsh frequently wind up being toned down. However, at the beginning, it is often better to start out on the tougher side. You can lighten up more easily than you can become tough.

Unfortunately, when the covenant is broken, the consequences must be enforced despite how difficult it may seem. Although you would much rather give warnings without end to prevent having to implement the punishment, the difficulty with multiple

EIGHT
eight
eIGHT
eight
eight
eight
EIGHT
eight
eIGHT
eight
eight
eight
EIGHT
eight
eIGHT
eight
eight
eight
EIGHT
eight
eIGHT
eight
eight
eight

EIGHT

eight

eIGHT

eight

eisht

eight

EIGHT

eight

eIGHT

eight

eisht

eight

EIGHT

eight

eIGHT

eight

eisht

eight

EIGHT

eight

eIGHT

eight

eisht

eight

warnings is that you are seen as someone who will not enforce the rules. That has two results. One, you are seen as a pushover; and two, the other youth, who actually want the covenant enforced and the objectionable behavior stopped, quickly become annoyed with you. Limit the number of warnings you give.

When the time comes to implement the consequences, enforce them calmly, without anger, no matter how difficult that may be. Now is not the time for yelling at a particular youth; losing control of your temper only undermines your authority. Try not to embarrass the offender publicly. If you must speak to a youth about his or her behavior and its disruptive influence, keep him or her after the program and talk with him or her privately. It is easy to lose your temper, especially when a youth knows how to punch every one of your buttons and has just done so. Nevertheless, the best thing you can do is to take a deep breath, count to ten, calmly let him or her know that his or her behavior is not appreciated, and suggest more positive expressions.

Parental Involvement

> How can young people keep their way pure? By guarding it according to your word.
> (Psalm 119:9, NRSV)

Finally, do not be afraid to involve parents. This is a chance to gain insight and support from parents in an effort to understand the cause of the behavior issues. Behavior problems may be a sign of difficulties at home or of a difficult situation elsewhere. Troubles in one area of life (school, home, friends, family) typically carry over into other areas as well, including youth group. Although such knowledge may not excuse the behavior, it may help you understand why it is occurring, opening the way for dialogue between you and the youth.

With a broader understanding, you are better able to deal with and resolve the behavior problems of the youth. Be sure that parents know the rules and the consequences as thoroughly as the youth do. They need to be prepared for a potential 3:00 a.m. wake-up call to come pick up a disruptive child from a lock-in.

Keep parents informed about their son's or daughter's positive behavior, not just the problems. Too often, parents do not hear the

good things their teenager has been doing. They may be pleasantly surprised to hear that the teenage son who has been giving them grief at home is the one who came up with the new youth group mission statement. Set up lines of support with parents by communicating with them. Parents may gain new insights into their youth with the information you have for them.

Checkpoints

❑ Inform parents of both negative and positive behaviors.
❑ Glean insights about the youth from the parents and the family situation.
❑ Ensure that parents know the rules and consequences.

Be sure that parents understand the covenant and consequences from the beginning. One of the simplest ways to do this is to send covenants home for both the youth and the parent to sign, well before an event takes place. Have a parent meeting at the beginning of the year, with periodic follow-up meetings throughout the year. Parents can be informed of the youth covenant, as well as find out about upcoming events, deadlines, and projects. Follow-up with parents also provides an opportunity for feedback. Communicating with parents keeps them informed about what is happening with the youth ministry and may help to gain their support for the youth activities and programs.

EIGHT
eight
eIGHT
eight
eight
eight
EIGHT
eight
eIGHT
eight
eight
eight
EIGHT
eight
eIGHT
eight
eight
eight
EIGHT
eight
eIGHT
eight
eight
eight

NINE
nine
NINe
nine
nine
nine
NINE
nine
NINe
nine
nine
nine
NINE
nine
NINe
nine
nine
nine

In January of each year, I put together my "Budget Notebook" to keep track of the youth ministry finances for the year. Since the church I work in has a youth ministry line item in the larger budget and a financial secretary, I typically submit receipts to her to pay for the ministry expenses. She keeps track of what has been spent and what remains in the budget. However, the youth ministry also has a checking account, separate from the rest of the budget, for which I keep receipts.

So, in my Budget Notebook, I have two major sections: one for the checking account, and one for the budget line item expenses. In the "checking account" section, I have separate areas for receipts and bank statements, plus a chart for keeping track of deposits and expenses. Also included in the chart are explanations of where deposits came from and why checks were written. Within the "line item" section are several charts: one each for "supplies," "programs," "curriculum," "retreats/counselor expenses," "confirmation," and "caring ministry." When I submit receipts to the financial secretary, I also keep track in my charts, along with why the money was spent.

Why go to all that trouble? So that I also take responsibility for keeping track of how much money is spent. I look at long-term planning by making sure that I still have money for the rest of the year. I justify the budget I request from the Finance Committee by the expenses from the previous year. I prove that I am being responsible with the budget I have been given and protect myself by keeping track of budget requests. In short, I am intentional about demonstrating what it means to be a good steward.

how to budget

Be a Responsible Steward of Resources

Planning a budget is not just for the financial secretary or the finance committee. You, too, must design a budget for your ministry area, whether it involves money that is part of a larger church budget, or money that is raised by the youth and sponsors through fundraising efforts.

Simply stated, a budget is a plan for spending specific amounts of money in certain areas so that ministry needs can be met over the course of the week, month, or year. A budget is a plan for future activities, a guideline for you and other church members to use in determining the framework of your ministry. A budget also shows your estimated costs and the fluctuations in expenses from year to year, and it can be helpful in determining your priorities and goals for the ministry.

Essentials for Budgeting

★ Use of a Budget

★ Identification of Priorities and Goals

★ Review and Estimation of Expenses

★ Evaluation and Adjustment of the Budget

Budgeting is not always fun, especially for "non-numbers people." However, you must budget when it comes to your ministries. In some churches, other ministry areas or church members can help make up the difference when unexpected shortfalls arise; however those situations are rare exceptions. You have to prove that you can be responsible with the funds with

nine
NINE
nine
NINe
nine
nine
nine
NINE
nine
NINe
nine
nine
nine
NINE
nine
NINe
nine
nine

NINE

nine

NiNe

nine

nine

nine

NINE

nine

NiNe

nine

nine

nine

NINE

nine

NiNe

nine

nine

nine

NINE

nine

NiNe

nine

nine

nine

which you are entrusted. You must make and meet your budget guidelines. Although no budget is perfect, through a spending plan, you show that you are a responsible steward and that you are capable of planning, compromising, and adapting as needed to achieve a healthy, thriving ministry.

Use of a Budget

> Now it is required that those who have been
> given a trust must prove faithful.
> (1 Corinthians 4:2, NIV)

Budgeting in ministry areas is important. Through budgets, you communicate your objectives for your ministry. By examining your budget, the church can easily see your major areas of concern and the financial support necessary to make them happen. This written communication with the church members helps them understand the priorities of the youth ministry and where financial assistance is needed. They can see where you are planning to spend your money over the next year, and how much you will need.

Checkpoints

❑ Use your budget to communicate your ministry objectives.
❑ Use your budget in planning.
❑ Use your budget to make cost-effective decisions.

In addition, setting a budget helps you plan your future ministries and programs. Knowing that you have a certain amount of funds available determines what is of primary importance to your ministry and allows you to adjust your plans and timing accordingly. By planning a yearly budget to coincide with the church's fiscal year, you know what total funds are available for the following year and how your programs connect with the other ministries in the church. Whether the youth ministry budget depends on fundraisers or is a part of the unified church budget, you know from the beginning how much money you need to achieve your goals.

Budgeting helps you plan cost-effectively. Although you do know that your financial resources are not infinite, seeing that information in plain black and white reminds you of your need to be careful in spending what you have allotted to your group. Just as your personal home budget helps you do long-range planning for costly items, having a budget for youth ministry helps you look ahead and balance your expenses over a longer period of time. When you have only a certain amount of funds, you certainly do not want to spend it all in the first few months of the year.

Identification of Priorities and Goals

> They are to do good, to be rich in good works, generous, and ready to share, thus storing up for themselves the treasure of a good foundation for the future.
>
> (1 Timothy 6:18-19, NRSV)

Before starting to write a budget, determine your specific funding needs. What must be paid out of this particular budget? Is the budget for only weekly youth fellowship meetings; or will it include confirmation classes, teacher training, Sunday school curriculum, and other materials? Keep your youth ministry's and your church's mission statements in mind. What programs and activities do you have in mind, and do they fit with your mission statement?

Consider what you hope to achieve over the course of the next year and what steps need to be taken in order to achieve those goals. Determine the most important aspects of the youth ministry you are seeking to fund. These may not be the items that require the most funds; but these are the programs that you know you want funded, regardless. These choices will be as different for each ministry as mission statements and groups differ from church to church.

Once you have identified what is most important to your ministry and best exemplifies your mission statement, determine what needs the most funding in your budget. By calculating which areas need to receive what percentage of your budget, you can then divide the funds accordingly. Considering what *needs* to be funded versus what you *want* funded helps to financially prioritize the different parts of your ministry. When faced with limited resources, you will know ahead of time what needs funding first and what can wait until another time or what can be funded by alternative means.

While you may wish the larger church budget could include money for all of the things you want to do and accomplish, keep

NINE
nine
NINe
nine
nine
nine

NINE
nine
NINe
nine
nine
nine

NINE
nine
NINe
nine
nine
nine

NINE
nine
NINe
nine
nine
nine

NINE

nine

NINe

nine

nine

nine

NINE

nine

NINe

nine

nine

nine

NINE

nine

NINe

nine

nine

nine

NINE

nine

NINe

nine

nine

nine

in mind that the economy swings back and forth between booms and recessions and that not all churches even include youth ministry as a line item in their budget. Being able to work with what you have is key for budgeting in youth ministry.

Checkpoints

❑ Consider what is most important to the ministry.
❑ Allocate resources to their best use.
❑ Keep records for future reference.

In addition to identifying your priorities and goals, keep records for future reference and for use by committees, chairpersons, and even other, future youth ministers. Having records of budgets and expenses from year to year is an enormous help for setting (and defending) future budgets. Keeping records enables you to learn from your mistakes from year to year and improve your budgeting skills as time goes on.

In addition, records of your expenses demonstrate that you are being a responsible steward. Data tables and receipt records protect you by documenting how your budget is spent and that it is not being misused. Keeping written records shows on paper what your ministry priorities are and where the majority of your budget is spent. (Note: Those might not be the same thing!)

Review and Estimation of Expenses

> Listen to advice and accept instruction, that you may gain wisdom for the future.
> (Proverbs 19:20, NRSV)

When planning a budget for the next year, start at the beginning. Look at the previous year's budget and expenses if they are available. A previous budget is a good place to start as a reference point. If this information is on hand, the budgeting process is a lot easier than when starting from scratch.

If possible, look at more than one year's information. Although costs and expenses vary from year to year, odds are that the increases and differences will not be drastic. However, several years' worth of budgeting information can show if certain years had unexpected or large expenses. Multiple expense sheets can show if previous years' budgets have been sufficient, or if expenses have consistently been higher or lower than estimated. This information gives you a better idea of the financial picture for the youth ministry. With a previous budget, some adjustments for inflation, and consideration of new programs and activities, you can determine the figures needed for the following year.

If a previous budget and list of expenses are not available, creating a brand-new budget is not impossible, just a little more work. When planning a budget without past figures to rely on, or when adding new things to a budget, a little homework and research is called for. Consider costs of materials, retreat locations, supplies, and extra for unexpected expenses. Think about including money for volunteer training, paying the way for adult chaperones, youth scholarships for trips, and "caring ministry" materials (thank-you notes, birthday cards, get well cards). Churches may or may not have office supplies and postage available for the youth ministry, so this may be yet another section of your budget.

Once you have thought through as many sub-categories in your youth ministry as possible and have researched estimated costs, you can use these numbers as a framework to build your budget. In lieu of past records, consider contacting other youth ministers at churches of similar size for information about their budgets. In addition to the estimates or past budget figures, assume some increase for inflation, then add extra for the unplanned occasions that will arise.

Checkpoints

❑ Learn from past budget information to determine future plans.
❑ Use estimates to provide a framework for the budget.
❑ Consider "big-ticket events."

Be sure to include "big-ticket events" in your estimates. These tend to consume a significant portion of your budget in a short amount of time. For example, while ordinary Sunday school curriculum, youth group supplies, and fellowship supper costs are spread out over the course of a year, confirmation curriculum, gifts, and supplies can quickly use a large portion of a budget in just a few months. Paying all or some of adult chaperone costs can use up budget funds during the summer when beach retreats, mission trips, theme park visits, or whitewater rafting excursions

NINE

nine

NINe

nine

nine

nine

NINE

nine

NINe

nine

nine

nine

NINE

nine

NINe

nine

nine

nine

NINE

nine

NINe

nine

nine

nine

NINE

nine

NINe

nine

nine

nine

NINE

nine

NINe

nine

nine

nine

NINE

nine

NINe

nine

nine

nine

NINE

nine

NINe

nine

nine

nine

are typically planned. This does not mean that you should not help pay for counselor costs (far from it), but that you should be sure to include those in your budget, and plan for those to occur at certain times. Likewise, if confirmation materials are part of your area, know and plan for the time when those costs will happen. Be sure to factor peak expense times into your budget.

Evaluation and Adjustment of the Budget

> Why spend money on what is not bread, and your labor on what does not satisfy?
>
> (Isaiah 55:2, NIV)

Once you have settled on a budget, periodically review your actual expenses. Are you on target with your estimates, or are you much higher or lower in certain areas? If you examine your expenses on a month-to-month basis, you can adjust quickly if expenses are growing more rapidly than you had originally planned. As you keep records of your expenses, you may wish to use an expense sheet to track your costs. (See the end of the chapter for a sample expense sheet.) Expense sheets keep your financial information at your fingertips, easily seen and shared as needed. It is far better to realize that your budget could be in trouble early on, when adjustments can be made, than to be over budget by the end of the year.

After reviewing your figures, as with any evaluation, you may need to adjust and make changes. Unless you have managed to be exactly on target with your estimated and actual expenses, adaptations to your ministry plan will need to happen. By referring to the priorities you set for your ministry in the budget-making process, you can decide what to cut or reduce to compensate for higher than expected costs. Based on your earlier assessment of the various aspects of your ministry you already know what programs you want to fund first, what can wait until a later time, and what can be funded through alternative plans.

Checkpoints

❑ Periodically review actual expenses.
❑ Adjust figures as needed.
❑ Compromise within your budget.

Alternative funding is especially important if a budget is cut, or the funds you raise are simply not enough to cover your estimated expenses. That does not always mean more fundraisers, however. Selling Easter lilies, having benefit suppers, selling emergency road kits, or holding car washes seem to be a staple of youth ministries; but there are other options.

If available, state- or conference-wide church resource centers will loan materials, including books and videos for a yearly fee. Advertise within the church if you need a particular movie for a youth program; odds are pretty good that someone may have it, saving your budget the rental fee.

If more fundraisers are called for, do your best to be creative and nonrepetitive. Unfortunately, school systems are relying more and more on fundraisers to cover their programs and trips; and many teenagers are simply burned out from selling so many different things.

Find out what is sold routinely from the schools in your area (wrapping paper, cookies, pizzas) and try to provide something different. As a different choice, you may want to go in a completely new direction, and not sell *something* but provide a service, such as raking leaves, painting houses, or babysitting. The list can be endless. If your creative juices are not flowing enough to come up with something new, talk to other youth ministers for suggestions, or check into your nearby Christian bookstore for books of ideas for fundraisers.

No budget is perfect. However, with careful planning, you can create a budget that fits most of your ministry needs. Even though budget-setting requires investing some of your own time and energy in setting goals and researching estimated costs, in the long run, the time is well worth it. You are called to be a responsible steward of the resources entrusted to you, whether as part of a larger church budget, or as raised by the youth and adult counselors. Even non-numbers people can create a budget and exercise effective use of resources.

NINE
nine
NINe
nine
nine
NINE
nine
NINe
nine
nine
nine
NINE
nine
NINe
nine
nine
nine
NINE
nine
NINe
nine
nine
nine

NINE
nine
NINe
nine
nine
nine
NINE
nine
NINe
nine
nine
nine
NINE
nine
NINe
nine
nine
nine
NINE
nine
NINe
nine
nine
nine

Sample Youth Ministry Budget Proposal

(Letter to the finance committee, for a church with youth ministry as a part of the unified budget)

Dear Finance Committee,

Previous Year's Budget for Youth Ministries = $3,500

Projected Next Year's Budget = $4,000

Like Children's Ministry, we have a great problem: We are growing! We average between 15 and 20 youth each week, up significantly from our average of 10 youth or fewer last year. Our main growth is in the junior high program. This year, a large number of sixth (or fifth) graders graduated into the youth ministry program, and almost all are active. Using figures from last year as a point of reference, I am projecting this breakdown for next year:

Supplies $750

(Program supplies, fall festival, photos, crafts)

spent last year = $650

Programs/UMYF Supper $750

(Lock-ins, programs, mileage, parent dinners, snack suppers)

spent last year = $675

Confirmation $1,200

(Includes: supplemental cost for confirmation retreat, class books, gifts)

spent last year = $900 for 5 confirmands

NINE

nine

NINe

nine

nine

nine

NINE

nine

NINe

nine

nine

nine

NINE

nine

NINe

nine

nine

nine

NINE

nine

NINe

nine

nine

nine

Curriculum $600

(Devotional magazines, program books, devotional
material, Sunday school materials)

        spent last year = $500

Retreats $450

(Ski trip, senior high and junior high retreats,
white-water rafting)

        spent last year = $350

Caring Ministry $250

(Birthday cards, Christmas cards, get well and
thinking of you bags, teacher gifts, Sunday
school teacher appreciation dinner)

        spent last year = $225

Total $4,000

Thank you for your consideration. If you have any questions
about these figures, please do not hesitate to ask me.

First Church Youth Minister

NINE
nine
NiNe
nine
nine
nine
NINE
nine
NiNe
nine
nine
nine
NINE
nine
NiNe
nine
nine
nine
NINE
nine
NiNe
nine
nine
nine

Sample Monthly Budget

Monthly Youth Budget

January	Curriculum	$	80
	Supplies	$	90
	Programs	$	60
	Confirmation	$	100
	Caring Ministry	$	65
	TOTAL	**$**	**395**

February	Curriculum	$	30
	Supplies	$	60
	Programs	$	60
	Confirmation	$	175
	Caring Ministry	$	15
	TOTAL	**$**	**340**

March	Curriculum	$	60
	Retreats	$	150
	Supplies	$	60
	Programs	$	60
	Confirmation	$	800
	Caring Ministry	$	15
	TOTAL	**$**	**1,145**

April	Curriculum	$	30
	Supplies	$	60
	Programs	$	60
	Confirmation	$	125
	Caring Ministry	$	15
	TOTAL	$	290

May	Curriculum	$	30
	Supplies	$	60
	Programs	$	60
	Caring Ministry	$	15
	TOTAL	**$**	**165**

June	Curriculum	$	50
	Supplies	$	60
	Programs	$	60
	Caring Ministry	$	15
	TOTAL	**$**	**185**

July	Curriculum	$	30
	Retreats	$	100
	Supplies	$	60
	Programs	$	60
	Caring Ministry	$	20
	TOTAL	**$**	**270**

August	Curriculum	$	80
	Supplies	$	60
	Programs	$	60
	Caring Ministry	$	20
	TOTAL	**$**	**220**

September	Curriculum	$	90
	Supplies	$	60
	Programs	$	90
	Caring Ministry	$	20
	TOTAL	**$**	**260**

October	Curriculum	$	30
	Supplies	$	60
	Programs	$	60
	Caring Ministry	$	15
	TOTAL	**$**	**165**

November	Curriculum	$	60
	Supplies	$	60
	Programs	$	60
	Caring Ministry	$	15
	TOTAL	$	195

December	Curriculum	$	30
	Retreats	$	200
	Supplies	$	60
	Programs	$	60
	Caring Ministry	$	20
	TOTAL	**$**	**370**

ANNUAL TOTAL $ 4,000

Sample Youth Ministry Expense Sheet

January–February 2004

Date	Description	Amount
01/15	Curriculum	$22.23
01/28	Youth fellowship	$61.37
02/04	Sunday school	$49.00
02/10	Youth devotional material	$39.95
02/15	Magazine subscriptions	$107.55
02/15	Confirmation	$172.07
02/15	Student, mentor, parent books	$75.26
02/28	Supplies	$75.00
02/28	Retreat	$520.00
Total		**$1,122.43**

NINE
nine
NINe
nine
nine
nine
NINE
nine
NINe
nine
nine
nine
NINE
nine
NINe
nine
nine
nine
NINE
nine
NINe
nine
nine
nine

TEN

ten

TEN

ten

ten

ten

TEN

ten

TeN

ten

ten

ten

TEN

ten

TeN

ten

ten

ten

I recently helped a friend put together a presentation about his mission trip to Mexico. He had spent ten days working on a school building, living with a local family, and visiting the surrounding area. His church had been a great support as he planned his trip, and he had planned a dinner and presentation to share his experience with the church members.

Years ago, he would have had slides created from his film and then pictures developed from those (an expensive process). Instead, now we took two rolls of film to be developed as photos, along with a photo CD (the photos in digital format on a CD-ROM). For the third roll of film, which had been developed in Mexico, we chose the specific pictures he wanted for the presentation; scanned them into the computer; and saved them to disk, converting the pictures to digital format as well.

We used Microsoft® PowerPoint® to put the photos in order. In this presentation application, we were able to crop the photos, focusing on areas we wanted to emphasize and brightening photos to show the school children in the shadowed classrooms. Instead of taking the photos as is, we were able to personalize them to better illustrate the mission. We even created a music video with the greatest portion of the pictures, timing them to change with the beat of the music. Overall, we made the presentation more interesting for today's audience.

We did need some additional technology. Since our computer had a CD burner, we put the music and the photos on one disk. When we presented, we also needed a laptop and video projector (which we borrowed from another church) to display the photos from the CD-ROM. His final presentation went very well and was highly enjoyed, thanks to the use of current technology.

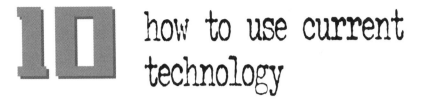

how to use current technology

Find the Benefits of Technology in the Church

> They were all amazed, and they kept asking one another, "What is this? A new teaching—with authority!"
>
> (Mark 1:27, NRSV)

Depending on your age, much of current technology may be somewhat new to you. Many of you may remember the days of the purple mimeograph machines and manual and electric typewriters. Others remember being taught in elementary school not only how to use, but how to program a computer, using simple programming languages. Then in the early 1980s, we learned to use MS-DOS, instead of programming language, to make the computer do what you wanted; and suddenly, telling the computer what you wanted it to do was much easier. Later, Windows, the Internet, and e-mail evolved, enabling us to keep in touch with our friends via notes sent through phone lines or computer cables. For today's teenagers, all of this technology is comfortable and familiar. They have grown up with computers, e-mail, instant messaging, the Internet, and the world at their fingertips.

Essentials for Using and Keeping Up With Current Technology

⭐ Word Processing and Desktop Publishing Software

⭐ Internet

⭐ Church Website With a Youth Page

⭐ E-mail and Instant Messaging

⭐ Presentation Software

⭐ Technical Assistance

ten
TEN
ten
TeN
ten
ten
ten
TEN
ten
TeN
ten
ten
ten
TEN
ten
TeN
ten
ten

TEN

ten

Ten

ten

ten

ten

TEN

ten

Ten

ten

ten

ten

TEN

ten

Ten

ten

ten

ten

TEN

ten

Ten

ten

ten

ten

Teenagers are accustomed to using much of today's software and are extremely Internet savvy. For them, computers and technology are a fact of life, something they are used to having always available. Adults also use computers on a daily basis, both at work and at home. The age range for computer-users spans generations, with grandchildren sending grandparents current photos via digital technology, and vice versa. Computers have become much easier to use; although like most things, practice helps even more. The easy availability of the Internet provides public access to information, which can be extremely beneficial when trying to reach out to the community. The myriad programs and uses for computers and technology allow nearly everyone to find something that works for his or her ministry.

Word Processing and Desktop Publishing Software

The ability to use a word processor and a desktop publishing application is almost a necessity for a youth minister. You can get by with using clip art and hand-written flyers, but today's teens are inundated with brightly colored and flashy advertising and television shows. You need to keep up. Inserting computer clip art and digital images into your document and creating fun layouts help your youth ministry newsletter stay interesting and eye-catching. You need to catch the youth's eye and their interest.

Another advantage to using word processing and desktop publishing is the ease of use. Many desktop publishing applications have step-by-step directions for assisting the user to create calendars, postcards, flyers, and banners. Also included are multiple graphics to insert into documents. The ability to modify a letter or calendar on a monthly basis is easier when you change the dates on the monthly calendar but leave your weekly Sunday night youth programs, weekly Bible study, and other regular events still in place. The advent of word processing makes it possible to keep your written records in digital form, saving on paper and storage.

Internet

The Internet is as important as word processing for youth ministers. The Internet provides a wealth of information about almost every possible topic. For example, typing the phrase *spiritual gifts* into one particular search engine found more than 2.5 million results, including sites designed to help the web surfer discover his or her own spiritual gifts. Granted, not all 2.5 million results have exactly what you are looking for; but for youth ministers in small towns or without access to a nearby Christian bookstore, the Internet can furnish a wide variety of information for programs from a variety of sources. Many denominations have websites as well, with information on the denomination's beliefs, where to find local churches, and news of importance to church members.

When looking at websites online, remember one thing: Building a website and uploading it on the Internet is so easy that anyone can do it. Look closely at the information presented. Is it correct? Is it theologically sound? Who created and posted the web page and what is his or her background? You certainly can use this information as research or a reference, but you cannot copy it any more than you can plagiarize from text resources.

In addition, while ordering resources through the Internet is easy and convenient, be careful if asked to provide credit card numbers or personal information. In an age of computer hackers and scam artists, that information could be used in ways you never intended.

Church Website With a Youth Page

In today's digital society, having a church website and youth web page is very important. Teenagers are online, surfing the Internet on a regular basis. Having your youth ministry information easily accessible makes it easier for them to find your church, your schedule, and important information about the ministry. Youth expect everything that they are interested in to have an online presence. They are especially interested in seeing themselves and information about them online, and information about their lives and their friends.

TEN
ten
TeN
ten
ten
ten
TEN
ten
TeN
ten
ten
ten
TEN
ten
TeN
ten
ten
ten
TEN
ten
TeN
ten
ten
ten

TEN
ten
Ten
ten
ten
ten
TEN
ten
Ten
ten
ten
ten
TEN
ten
Ten
ten
ten
ten
TEN
ten
Ten
ten
ten
ten

Newcomers to your area can look at websites to locate a church even before coming to town. Having a church website provides an opportunity for anyone to learn about your church, its members, its mission statement, and available ministries. For example, learning that a church has a youth ministry program may be the point of interest that will bring that family to your church and to the youth ministry. Websites can be a method of publicity so widespread that people from around the world can learn about your church.

A website helps you keep in touch with college students. Posting the church newsletter on the Internet enables them to know what is happening in the life of the church (while saving the church money in postage). Some churches have an online Sunday school class for their college students, reaching their students from across the state and across the country and aiding in continued spiritual growth, even after they have graduated from your youth ministry program.

Simple, clear websites are the easiest to navigate and to read. Although pictures are exciting and liven up a web page, too many can slow the site down when someone comes to browse the site. Read some books on how to design a web page, and take advantage of free Web space if it is available through your denomination.

Caution: Be careful to keep personal information about your youth and church members off the page. While printing first names may be acceptable, listing last names and addresses should never be done for any member, but especially not for underage teenagers.

E-mail and Instant Messaging

E-mail has not completely replaced the physical presence of a youth newsletter or birthday card, but the convenience of e-mail is another necessity for youth ministry. Phone calls are wonderful for an immediate response when the person is home; but with today's teenager's hectic schedules, actually finding a teenager at home is almost impossible. Many teenagers have e-mail accounts, which they check frequently. You can write your e-mail to all of them at once and they can respond when they have time—even when it is midnight and you have already gone to bed. Free e-mail accounts are available in a variety of places, including Hotmail.com, Yahoo.com, and Juno.com. As a youth minister, you *must* have an active e-mail account.

You can get even quicker responses through instant messaging (IM). AOL, Yahoo, ICQ, MSN, and others have free instant messaging services available to anyone with Internet access, whether or not you are a member of that particular Internet service provider. Instant messaging even seems to have its own language when writing to others, mainly phonetic abbreviations of words for quicker typing and responses. Make a point to learn the lingo of instant messaging. Many teenagers spend hours online, chatting with friends, often chatting with several at a time.

When you become savvy in the language of instant messaging, you may want to have a IM Bible study or talk time where your youth can ask questions and you answer on the spot.

A few cautions for e-mail and instant messaging: As with all writing, facial expressions and voice tones cannot be expressed in type. For example, sarcasm is not readable in writing unless you alert the recipient directly that you are, in fact, being sarcastic. Be careful what you type so that your words are not misinterpreted. Guard against your writing being misunderstood by others.

Another thing to remember is that your e-mails and instant messages are written text, not spoken words. Do not write anything that you are not willing to have as a permanent record. Instant message conversations and e-mails can be saved and printed. If a joke is being misinterpreted, those comments could be held against you. Using good judgment and keeping statements simple may not prevent all misunderstandings but certainly will reduce the number.

Presentation Software

Microsoft® PowerPoint®, MediaShout®, and other presentation software make the traditional youth ministry talk more appealing to today's teenager. This generation has grown up on MTV videos, with flash, glitz, style, and music. A simple lecture-style discussion is not going to work with them. Presentation software uses slides but makes the traditional slide machine or overhead

TEN
ten
TeN
ten
ten
ten
TEN
ten
TeN
ten
ten
ten
TEN
ten
TeN
ten
ten
ten
TEN
ten
TeN
ten
ten
ten

TEN
ten
Ten
ten
ten
ten
TEN
ten
Ten
ten
ten
ten
TEN
ten
Ten
ten
ten
ten
TEN
ten
Ten
ten
ten
ten

projector obsolete. With a presentation application, you can insert movie scenes, clip art, sound, movement, and photographs into your talks. If you want to use a certain scene in a movie as an example, instead of describing the scene, you can actually show the clip. Many teenagers today want an attention-grabbing experience. A good presentation software can help you do that.

You will also want to use the software to project music for worship and youth group. Learn to time digital slides so that they run automatically. Add images, art, and color lyric slides. With the slides moving on their own, you are free to direct, accompany the group, or participate. Remember that when using any copyrighted material, be sure to give the proper credit and get the proper permissions to show good stewardship and avoid legal problems.

In order to project the presentation, you will need a screen or blank wall, an LCD projector, and the presentation software on a computer. A laptop computer is most commonly used for running the presentations, even for worship services, due to the ease of moving the laptop computer from place to place. The equipment is not cheap but is well worth the expense to fully engage your youth. A less costly option would be to borrow the necessary equipment from a business, church member, or other community resource.

Technical Assistance

Obviously, you are going to need help to do all these things, especially if they are new to you. Many books can be found at the public library or basic bookstore on computers, and computer skills. Both the Complete Idiot's Guide series and the " ... for Dummies" series include books on many areas of expertise in computers.

Still, no matter how well a book may explain ways to set up a website or to create your first presentation slide, you will probably need to have guidance when trying it for the first time. Local community colleges offer courses on basic computer skills, as well as more advanced curriculum, including building websites, and making PowerPoint® presentations.

You probably have someone in your church who can help you with computer problems or will even agree to be your "techie" and put together and run your presentations. You can also check your youth group for experts. Some schools require students to do PowerPoint® presentations for class, and basic computer skills is usually a required course. Your youth probably know more than you do about the computers you are using. This is nothing to be ashamed of; this is an opportunity to help your youth find areas of service and ministry in the church.

Technology is here to stay, although it will continue to adapt and change as time goes on. Instead of resisting the influx of the digital age, you can find and use many aspects of the newer technology to help you in your ministry. Just as mimeograph machines replaced carbon paper, and photocopiers replaced mimeograph machines, today's word processors and desktop publishing software have replaced the typewriter and paste-ups. Digital technology can make your job easier, quicker, and more appealing to new generations. You have an opportunity to adapt and evolve with the youth, using their cultural media to reach them where they are and bring them closer to God.

TEN
ten
TeN
ten
ten
ten

TEN
ten
TeN
ten
ten
ten

TEN
ten
TeN
ten
ten
ten

TEN
ten
TeN
ten
ten
ten

reflection questions

ten
things

**TEN
THINGS**

ten
things

TeN
THINGS

ten
things

ten
things

ten
things

**TEN
THINGS**

ten
things

TeN
THINGS

ten
things

ten
things

ten
things

**TEN
THINGS**

ten
things

Chapter 1

- In what ways are you intentional about nurturing your spirituality?
- What do you see as major benefits of spending personal time with God in prayer and study?
- Who are your spiritual friends?
- Make a plan for participating in some acts of service. What kinds of projects do you enjoy? What agencies are near you for which you could offer a day to work?

Chapter 2

- What do you look for when you seek volunteers?
- How would you define a "high-quality" adult volunteer, based on what you read in Chapter 2?
- When was the last time you affirmed the work of your volunteers? Write their names on separate pieces of paper and list the reasons you are thankful for them and the positive things they do for the youth ministry. Then make a list of how you will make sure that they know how valuable they are to the ministry.

Chapter 3

- What is your youth ministry's mission statement? Why is it important that your volunteers agree with the mission and find a role within it?
- If you don't have job descriptions for your current volunteers, make one for each of them and meet with them to talk about whether they think it is accurate. Invite them to help you articulate expectations, roles, and responsibilities.

Chapter 4

- Are all of your volunteers working successfully? If you're feeling frustrated with one of your volunteers, make an appointment to talk to him or her about whether his or her gifts match the needs of the youth ministry.

Chapter 5

• Are you in the process of making a change right now? How might this chapter help you be effective? Follow the steps for implementing change and make sure to adapt as necessary.

Chapter 6

• How did you relate to the stories of dealing with difficult people?
• In what ways can you demonstrate Christian love when you are in conflict with someone?

Chapter 7

• Make a list of topics that you think your youth would like to discuss. Then have the youth submit some topics. When you have a good list, find a curriculum that will help you teach the topics so that you don't have to do all the work yourself.
• Reflect on what resistance you might have to the tougher topics. What can you do now to ward off fears or negative feelings?

Chapter 8

• What is your current style of discipline? How has this chapter helped you to think about disciplining in a Christian manner?
• Get a group together to write a youth group covenant.

Chapter 9

• How will you implement the process of budgeting talked about in this chapter?
• What are the benefits of modeling good stewardship?

Chapter 10

• How do you see e-mail and instant messaging as an asset to your youth ministry?
• What do you need to do to enhance or create a website?
• Make a list of youth and adults who could be your tech support team.

TeN things
TEN THINGS
TeN things
TeN THINGS
ten things
ten things
TeN things
TEN THINGS
TeN things
TeN THINGS
ten things
ten things
TeN things
TEN THINGS
TeN things
TeN THINGS
ten things
ten things

for more information and further reading

ten
things
TEN
THINGS
ten
things
TeN
THINGS
ten
things
ten
things
ten
things
TEN
THINGS
ten
things
TeN
THINGS
ten
things
ten
things
ten
things
TEN
THINGS
ten
things

Antagonists in the Church: How to Identify and Deal With Destructive Conflict, by Kenneth C. Haugk (Augsburg Fortress Publishers, 1988; ISBN: 0806623101). Publisher's description: "Antagonism exists in the church. It leaves in its wake broken lives: people who are hurt, discouraged, and apathetic. Although only a very few persons are antagonists, these individuals have the potential to disrupt and even destroy a congregation's mission and ministry."

Beyond the Ordinary: Spirituality for Church Leaders, by Ben Campbell Johnson and Andrew Dreitcer (William B. Eerdmans Publishing Company, 2001; ISBN: 0802847730). Written for church leaders who don't have training in spiritual formation, this is a look at the meaning of spirituality as it relates to leadership and to ministry.

The Budget-Building Book for Nonprofits: A Step-by-Step Book for Managers and Boards, by Murray Dropkin and Bill LaTouche (Jossey-Bass, 1998; ISBN: 0787940364). This book contains more than you could possibly want to know about creating a budget. It is very helpful for nonprofit businesses; some things are applicable to the church.

Carolina Cross Connection 2001 Camper Preparation Manual, (Carolina Cross Connection, P.O. Box 1457, Lincolnton, North Carolina, 28093-0457; *www.cross-connection.org*). A week-long mission experience in western North Carolina aimed at bringing youth and adults together in a Christian community so that the youth can practice leadership skills and grow in spiritual maturity, while spreading the love of Christ to people in need through service.

The Complete Idiot's Guide to Computer Basics (2nd Edition), by Joe Kraynak (Alpha Books, 2001; ISBN: 0028642309). Publisher's description: "Simple lessons to start 'newbies,' or inexperienced computer users, off on the path to computer proficiency. Offers steps for setting up a computer for maximum efficiency, and for making computer use more fun and less frustrating. Explains Windows, Web surfing, and other popular computer activities."

The Complete Idiot's Guide to Creating a Web Page (5th Edition), by Paul McFedries, (Alpha Books, 2002; ISBN: 002864316X). Publisher's description: This book "provides you with the tools you need to create and customize your web pages. A careful, step-by-step approach enables you to build and publish your first web page. With the basics in place, you are slowly introduced to more advanced concepts such as tables, forms, frames, and style sheets. Many examples illustrate each new concept, and you are encouraged to use and build upon these examples. Many new web page concepts are covered, including XML, style sheets, and JavaScript programs."

Conflict Management in Congregations, edited by David B. Lott (The Alban Institute, 2001; ISBN: 1566992435). A more general approach to dealing with conflicts that can divide congregations.

Controversial Discussion Starters, by Stephen Parolini (Group Publishing, 1992; ISBN: 1559451564). For youth ministry, this book uses a debate approach, presenting at least two sides to such difficult topics as euthanasia, abortion, social drinking, and cheating.

Coping With Difficult People, by Robert M. Bramson, Ph.D. (Dell Publishing, 1981; ISBN: 0440202019). A more thorough look at difficult people, including the labeling of the different kinds of difficult people often encountered, and individualized approaches for dealing with them.

Essential Managers: Managing Budgets, by Stephen Brookson (Dorling Kindersley, 2000; ISBN: 0789459698). A short, concise guide mainly designed for the business world, but with some helpful information.

Faith-Forming Junior High Ministry: Beyond Pizza 101, by Drew Dyson (Abingdon Press, 2003; ISBN: 0687075394). A breakthrough book causing you to think theologically about your ministry with junior high youth.

Feeding Your Soul: A Quiet Time Handbook, by Jean Fleming (NavPress, 1999; ISBN: 1576831442). This is an excellent practical

109

ten
things
TEN
THINGS
ten
things

Ten
THINGS

ten
things

ten
things

ten
things
TEN
THINGS
ten
things

Ten
THINGS

ten
things

ten
things

ten
things
TEN
THINGS
ten
things

Ten
THINGS

ten
things

ten
things

guide to the how and why of establishing daily devotional time and its importance in your relationship with God.

Great Fundraising Ideas for Youth Groups, edited by David and Kathy Lynn (Youth Specialties/Zondervan, 1993; ISBN: 031067171X). This book includes more than 150 great, easy ideas for the creatively challenged. It includes chapters on ethical fundraising.

How to Deal With Difficult People (Successful Office Series), by Donald H. Weiss (American Management Association, 1987; ISBN: 0814476740). This is a concise look at difficult people and gives helpful advice for dealing with them.

How to Mobilize Church Volunteers, by Marlene Wilson (Augsburg Fortress Publishers, 1990; ISBN: 0806620129). The author, an international authority on volunteerism, says, "Problems in any church's volunteer program can be corrected. We can learn to care as much about people as we do about programs by using sound principles for human resource management." This helpful book includes appendices with sample job descriptions, characteristics of a servant/leader, questionnaires, and interest sheets.

How to Train Volunteer Teachers: 20 Workshops for the Sunday School, by Delia Touchton Halverson (Abingdon Press, 1991; ISBN: 0687179750). Although this book is aimed at workshops for Sunday school teachers, many of the topics can be transferred to youth group leaders as well.

The Internet for Dummies (9th Edition), by John R. Levine, Carol Baroudi, and Margaret Levine Young (John Wiley and Sons, 2003; ISBN: 0764541730). This guide to using the Internet, for beginners, shows how to surf the web, send e-mail, chat, use instant messaging, and more.

Low Cost, No Cost Ideas for Youth Ministry (Group Publishing, Inc., 1994; ISBN: 1559451874). This book gives many ideas for stretching budgets, with fundraisers, games, Bible studies, trips, and more.

New Tools for a New Century: First Steps in Equipping Your Church for the Digital Revolution, by John P. Jewell, Jr. (Abingdon Press, 2002; ISBN: 0687045479). This excellent guide gives practical advice on how to get started with a computer, then doing everything from setting up a website or using presentation software—all ways to use digital technology in the church.

Nurturing the Soul of the Youth Worker: 8 Ways to Energize Your Life and Ministry, by Tim Smith (Group Publishing, Inc., 1999; ISBN: 0764421352). This book introduces ways to "keep your soul on fire" and to develop your spirituality and character. Even though the lessons tend to focus more on the youth than on the youth worker, they are applicable to adults too.

Positive Discipline in the Classroom: Developing Mutual Respect, Cooperation, and Responsibility in Your Classroom (Revised 2rd Edition), by Jane Nelsen, Ed.D.; and Lynn Lott, M.A; and H. Stephen Glenn, Ph.D. (Prima Publishing, 2000; ISBN: 0761524215). This book is part of a series on Positive Discipline. Even though this book was written for teachers; it has useful ideas for youth ministers.

Positive Discipline for Teenagers: Empowering Your Teens and Yourself Through Kind and Firm Parenting (Revised 3rd Edition), by Jane Nelsen, Ed.D. and Lynn Lott, M.A. (Prima Publishing, 2000; ISBN: 076152181X). This book is part of a series on Positive Discipline. Even though this book was written for parents, it has applicable ideas for anyone who works with youth.

Purpose-Driven® Youth Ministry, by Doug Fields (Zondervan, 1998; ISBN: 0310212537). This book, intended for creating and maintaining a youth ministry with a purpose, includes a "helpful approach to building a self-sustaining youth ministry."

Sabbath Time: Understanding the Practice for Contemporary Christians (Revised Edition), by Tilden Edwards (Upper Room Books, 2003; ISBN: 0835898628). Edwards helps the reader understand why Sabbath time is important and necessary to the contemporary Christian.

Sacred Bridges: Making Lasting Connections Between Older Youth and the Church, by Mike Ratliff (Abingdon Press, 2002; ISBN: 0687063663). *Sacred Bridges* provides help for pastors, youth leaders, and other adults who are interested in keeping senior high youth involved in church. The book offers success stories from churches who have not only retained youth but have reached new youth in the high school years. From these success stories,

ten
things
TEN
THINGS
ten
things
TeN
THINGS
ten
things
ten
things
ten
things
TEN
THINGS
ten
things
TeN
THINGS
ten
things
ten
things
ten
things
TEN
THINGS
ten
things
TeN
THINGS
ten
things
ten
things

Mike Ratliff distills the principles that will enable other churches to be more effective in reaching and keeping senior high youth.

Sage Advice: Stories From seasoned Youth Workers, by Scott Gillenwaters, with Richard Bardusch, Jane Currin, John O'Kain, and Blair Waddell (Abingdon Press, 2003; ISBN: 0687051878). This book is a tell-all of true stories from veteran youth workers. Some stories will make you laugh out loud, others will make you think, and some could even make you cry.

Who Moved My Cheese? An Amazing Way to Deal With Change in Your Work and in Your Life, by Spencer Johnson, MD. (G.P. Putnam's Sons, 1998; ISBN: 0399144463). A brief tale of how people react to change, as seen through the eyes of two mice and two humans.

Youth Ministry Management Tools, by Ginny Olson, Diane Elliot, and Mike Work (Zondervan, 2001; ISBN: 0310235960). In this extensive resource, you'll find tools to help you manage yourself and your ministry, as well as help you stay in youth ministry, including a CD-ROM with sample forms and checklists.

Many church denominations have Social Creeds, Social Principles, or some type of written statements on their stance on various issues, which can be helpful to review and to know before presenting these topics to your youth group.

Websites

www.ileadyouth.com. This site is a searchable index of relevant topics for youth groups and includes pertinent youth ministry articles and downloadable lessons for immediate use.

www.youthspecialties.com. This site offers the most complete youth worker job search available. It also highlights youth resources, regional workshops, and national events.

If you would like a checklist of all of the checkpoints (❑) items in this book, e-mail youth@abingdonpress.com and ask for the *10 Things* Checkpoints.